Nick Vandome

Laptops
for Seniors

in easy steps

Windows 8 edition

In easy steps is an imprint of In Easy Steps Limited
4 Chapel Court · 42 Holly Walk · Leamington Spa
Warwickshire · United Kingdom · CV32 4YS
www.ineasysteps.com

Notice of Liability
Every effort has been made to ensure that this book contains accurate
and current information. However, In Easy Steps Limited and the
author shall not be liable for any loss or damage suffered by readers
as a result of any information contained herein.

Trademarks
Microsoft® and Windows® are registered trademarks of Microsoft
Corporation. All other trademarks are acknowledged as belonging to
their respective companies.

In Easy Steps Limited supports The Forest Stewardship Council (FSC),
the leading international forest certification organisation. All our titles
that are printed on Greenpeace approved FSC certified paper carry the
FSC logo.

Mixed Sources
Product group from well-managed
forests and other controlled sources
www.fsc.org Cert no. SGS-COC-005998
© 1996 Forest Stewardship Council

FSC

Printed and bound in the United Kingdom

ISBN 978-1-84078-579-1

Contents

6 It's a Digital World 123

7 On Vacation 145

8 Sharing with Your Family 155

1 Choosing a Laptop

More and more computer users are now using laptops because of their convenience and portability. This chapter looks at some of the issues to consider when buying a laptop and how to ensure you buy the right one for your needs. It also covers the elements of a laptop and some of the accessories you will need.

A Brief History of Laptops

Modern computers have come a long way since the days of mainframe computers that took up entire rooms and were generally only the domain of large educational establishments or government organizations. Before microprocessors (the chips that are used to run modern-day computers) these mainframe computers were usually operated by punch-cards: the operators programmed instructions via holes in a punch-card and then waited for the results, which could take hours or days.

The first personal computers, i.e. ones in which all of the computing power was housed in a single box, started to appear in the early 1970s and the first machine that bore any resemblance to modern personal computers was called the Datapoint 2200. The real breakthrough for personal computers came with the introduction of microprocessors – small chips that contained all of the necessary processing power for the computer. After this, the industry expanded at a phenomenal rate with the emergence of major worldwide companies such as Microsoft, Apple, IBM, Dell and Intel.

But even as soon as personal computers were being developed for a mass-market audience, there was a concerted drive to try and create a portable computer so that people could take their own computer with them wherever they went. Even in the fast-moving world of technology the timescale for shrinking a computer from the size of a large room to the size of a small briefcase was a dramatic one.

First portable computers

With most types of technology we are obsessed with the idea of making the item as small as possible, whether it is a music player, a telephone or a computer. However, the first portable computers bore little resemblance to the machines that we now know as laptops. At the beginning of the 1980s there were a few portable computers released, but most of them were bulky, had very small screens and could not run on internal batteries. The most popular of these was called the Osborne 1, which was released in 1981. Although this

Don't forget

Apple has an excellent range of laptops, running its OS X operating system. However, the majority of this book deals with "IBM-compatible" laptops, as they are known. These types of laptops are the most common and run on the Windows operating system.

was the size of a small suitcase and had a minuscule amount of computing power compared with modern machines, it proved a big success as it enabled people to carry their computers around with them for the first time.

The machine that first used the term "laptop" was called the Gallian SC, which was developed in 1983 and introduced in 1984. This had the big advantage of being able to run on an internal battery and it was also one of the first portable computers that appeared with the now-universal "clamshell" design, where the monitor folded down over the keyboard.

In the late 1980s companies such as Kyocera, Tandy, Olivetti, NEC, IBM, Toshiba, Compaq and Zenith Data Systems began developing fast and more powerful laptops and it is in this period that the growth of laptops really began to take off.

In 1991 Apple introduced its PowerBook range of laptops and in 1995 the introduction of Windows 95 provided an operating system for IBM-compatible laptops.

Laptops have now become an integral part of the computer market and in many areas sales have outstripped those of desktop computers. Also, they are more than capable of comfortably meeting the computing needs of most computer users. Add to this their portability (which has reached a stage where you no longer need to worry about doing yourself an injury in order to carry one around) and it is clear why laptops have become so popular.

Mobility is now an essential part of computing: with the release of Windows 8, which is aimed firmly at the mobile world, it is clear that this is a key area for future development. Windows 8 is designed for traditional computers but also mobile devices with touch screen functionality. This is likely to be a growth area for laptops, with more and more manufacturers looking to provide devices which incorporate touch screens for navigating around a laptop's interface.

Don't forget

Because of their size and weight, the first portable computers, such as the Osborne 1, were known rather unflatteringly as "luggables".

Don't forget

Windows 8 is a considerable departure from previous versions of the Windows operating system and it is looked at in depth throughout the book.

9

Laptops v. Desktops

When considering buying a laptop computer one of the first considerations is how it will perform in comparison with a desktop computer. In general, you will pay more for a laptop with similar specifications to a desktop. The reason for this is purely down to size: it is more expensive to fit the required hardware into a laptop than the more generous physical capacity of a desktop computer. However, with modern computing technology and power, even laptops with lower specifications than their desktop cousins will be able to handle all but the most intensive computing needs of most home users. The one situation where laptops will have to have as high a specification as possible is if you are going to be doing a lot a video downloading and editing, such as converting and editing old family movies.

Some of the issues to consider when looking at the differences between laptops and desktops are:

- **Portability.** Obviously, laptops easily win over desktops in this respect but when looking at this area it is worth thinking about how portable you actually want your computer to be. If you want to mainly use it in the home then you may think that a desktop is the answer. However, a laptop gives you portability in the home too, which means that you can use your computer in a variety of locations within the home and even in the garden, if desired

- **Power.** Even the most inexpensive laptops have enough computing power to perform most of the tasks that the majority of users require. However, if you want to have the same computing power as the most powerful desktops, then you will have to pay a comparatively higher price

- **Functionality.** Again, because of their size, desktops have more room for items such as DVD writers, multi-card readers and webcams. These can be included with laptops but this can also increase the price and the weight of the laptop

Don't forget

Another issue with laptops is battery power, which is required to keep them operating when they are removed from a mains electrical source. Obviously, this is not an issue that affects desktops.

Types of Laptops

To meet the needs of the different groups who use laptops there are several variations that are available:

- **Netbooks.** These are the ultimate in small laptops, but have less power and functionality than larger options. They generally have screens that are approximately 10 inches (measured diagonally from corner to corner) and are best suited for surfing the web and sending email, although they can also do productivity tasks

- **Ultrabooks.** These are very light and slim laptops which still have significant power and functionality. They have screens of approximately 13 inches and weigh as little as 1.2 kg. They are an excellent option if you are going to be using your laptop a lot while traveling

- **Notebooks.** These are the most common types of laptops as they have a good combination of size, weight and power. They generally have screens that are approximately 13–17 inches and weigh approximately 2–3.5 kg. These are an excellent option for using in the home and also while traveling

- **Desktop replacements.** These are larger, heavier laptops that can be used in the home instead of a desktop computer. They are more powerful than other types of laptops but the downside is that they are not as portable. They generally have screens that are up to approximately 17–19 inches and weigh approximately 4–6 kg

- **Hybrids.** With the proliferation of touch screen mobile computing devices, such as smartphones and tablet computers, manufacturers have been looking at ways to incorporate this into laptops. This is being done with touch screen laptops and also hybrid devices that can be used as a laptop and also a tablet. This is done by including a keyboard that can be hidden (through techniques such as having a sliding or revolving screen) so that the device can also be used as a touch screen tablet. These devices run Windows 8 and are likely to become increasingly popular in the future

Beware

Netbooks usually have a slimmed-down version of the full Windows operating system, due to limits to their memory and architecture.

Don't forget

A lot of the weight in a laptop is taken up by peripherals such as DVD writers, card readers and webcams. The more of these that a laptop has, the heavier it is likely to be.

Laptop Jargon Explained

Since laptops are essentially portable computers, much of the jargon is the same as for a desktop computer. However, it is worth looking at some of this jargon and the significance it has in terms of laptops.

- **Processor.** Also known as the central processing unit, or CPU, this refers to the processing of digital data as it is provided by programs on the computer. The more powerful the processor, the quicker the data is interpreted

- **Memory.** This closely relates to the processor and is also known as random-access memory, or RAM. Essentially, this type of memory manages the programs that are being run and the commands that are being executed. The more memory there is, the quicker programs will run. With more RAM they will also be more stable and less likely to crash. In the current range of laptops, memory is measured in megabytes (MB) or gigabytes (GB)

- **Storage.** This refers to the amount of digital information that the laptop can store. In the current range of laptops storage is measured in gigabytes. There are no external signs of processor or memory on a laptop but the details are available from within the Computer option, which is accessed from the File Manager

Don't forget

Memory can be thought of as a temporary storage device as it only keeps information about the currently-open programs. Storage is more permanent as it keeps the information even when the laptop has been turned off.

12

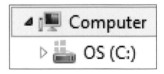

▲ Hard Disk Drives (2)

OS (C:)

57.7 GB free of 99.7 GB

- **Optical drive.** This is a drive on the laptop that is capable of reading information from, and copying it onto, a disc such as a CD or a DVD. Most modern laptops have internal optical drives such as CD writers or DVD writers

- **Connectivity.** This refers to the different types of media device to which the laptop can be connected. These include card readers for cards from digital cameras, USB devices such as music players, and FireWire devices such as digital video cameras

- **Graphics card.** This is a device that enables images, video and animations to be displayed on the laptop. It is also sometimes known as a video card. The faster the graphics card, the better the quality the relevant media will be displayed at. In general, very fast graphics cards are really only needed for intensive multimedia applications such as video games or videos

- **Wireless.** This refers to a laptop's ability to connect wirelessly to a network, i.e. another computer or an Internet connection. In order to be able to do this, the laptop must have a wireless card, which enables it to connect to a network or high-speed Internet connection

- **Ports.** These are the parts of a laptop into which external devices can be plugged, using a cable such as a USB. They are usually located on the side of the laptop and there can be two or three of each

- **Pointing device.** This is the part of the laptop that replaces the traditional mouse as a means of moving the cursor on the screen. Most pointing devices are in the form of a touch pad, where a finger on a pad is used to move the cursor. An external mouse can also be connected to a laptop and used in the conventional way

- **Webcam.** This is a type of camera that is fitted into the laptop and can be used to take still photographs or communicate via video with other people

Hot tip

External optical drives can also be connected to a laptop through a USB cable.

Don't forget

For more on using wireless technology see Chapter Nine.

Don't forget

USB stands for Universal Serial Bus and is a popular way of connecting external devices to computers.

Size and Weight

The issues of size and weight are integral to the decision to buy a laptop. In addition to getting a machine with enough computing power it is also important to ensure that the screen is large enough for your needs and that it is light enough for you to carry around comfortably.

Size

The main issue with the size of a laptop is the dimension of the screen. This is usually measured in inches, diagonally from corner to corner. The range for the majority of laptops currently on the market is approximately 12–17 inches, with some more powerful models going up to 19 inches.

When considering the size of screen it is important to think about how you are going to use your laptop:

- If you are going to use it mainly for functions such as letter writing and sending email then a smaller screen might suffice

- If you are going to use it mainly for functions such as surfing the web or editing and looking at photographs then you may feel more comfortable with a larger screen

- If you, or anyone else, is going to be using it for playing games and watching videos then the larger the screen, the better

Weight

Unless you are buying a laptop to replace a desktop, weight should not be too much of an issue as most models are similar in this respect. However, make sure you physically feel the laptop before you buy it.

If you are going to be traveling a lot with your laptop then a lighter, ultrabook type, may be the best option. When considering this take into account the weight of any type of case that you will use to carry the laptop as this will add to the overall weight.

Beware

Looking at material on a smaller screen can be more tiring on the eyes as, by default, it is displayed proportionally smaller than on a larger screen. It is possible to change the size of the screen display, but this will lead to less material being displayed on the screen. See Chapter Two to see how to change the screen display size.

Getting Comfortable

Since you will probably be using your laptop in more than one location, the issue of finding a comfortable working position can be vital, particularly as you cannot put the keyboard and monitor in different positions as you can with a desktop computer. Whenever you are using your laptop try and make sure that you are sitting in a comfortable position, with your back well supported, and that the laptop is in a position where you can reach the keyboard easily and also see the screen without straining.

Despite the possible temptation to do so, avoid using your laptop in bed, on your lap, or where you have to slouch or strain to reach the laptop properly:

Don't forget

Working comfortably at a laptop involves a combination of a good chair, good posture and good positioning of the laptop.

Hot tip

If possible, the best place to work at a laptop is at a dedicated desk or workstation.

15

Seating position

The ideal way to sit at a laptop is with an office-type chair that offers good support for your back. Even with these types of chairs it is important to maintain a good body position so that your back is straight and your head is pointing forwards.

If you do not have an office-type chair, use a chair with a straight back and place a cushion behind you for extra support and comfort as required.

Hot tip

One of the advantages of office-type chairs is that the height can usually be adjusted, and this can be a great help in achieving a comfortable position.

...cont'd

Laptop position

When working at your laptop it is important to have it positioned so that both the keyboard and the screen are in a comfortable position. If the keyboard is too low then you will have to slouch or strain to reach it:

If the keyboard is too high, your arms will be stretching. This could lead to pain in your tendons:

The ideal setup is to have the laptop in a position where you can sit with your forearms and wrists as level as possible while you are typing on the keyboard:

Beware

Take regular breaks when working with a laptop and stop working if you experience aches, or pins and needles in your arms or legs.

Adjusting the screen

Another factor in working comfortably at a laptop is the position of the screen. Unlike with a desktop computer, it is not feasible to have a laptop screen at eye level, as this would result in the keyboard being in too high a position. Instead, once you have achieved a comfortable seating position, open the screen so that it is approximately 90 degrees from your eye line:

Don't forget

Find a comfortable body position and adjust your laptop's position to this, rather than vice versa.

One problem with laptop screens is that they can reflect glare from sunlight or indoor lighting:

Beware

Most modern laptops have screens with an anti-glare coating. However, even this will not be very effective against bright sunlight that is shining directly onto the screen.

If this happens, either change your position, or block out the light source using some form of blind or shade. Avoid squinting at a screen that is reflecting glare as this will quickly give you a headache.

Carrying a Laptop

As laptops are designed for mobility, it is safe to assume that they will have to be carried around at some point. Because of the weight of even the lightest laptops, it can be uncomfortable to carry a laptop for any length of time. To try and minimize this, it is important to follow a few rules:

- Carry the laptop with a carry case that is designed for this task

- Carry the laptop on one side of your body and move it from side to side if necessary

- Do not cross the strap over your shoulders and try not to carry too many other items at the same time

If you are traveling with your laptop you might be able to incorporate it into your luggage, particularly if it can be moved on wheels.

Keyboard and Mouse

Laptops have the same basic data input devices as desktop computers, i.e. a keyboard and a mouse. A laptop keyboard is very similar to a desktop one, although it is best to try the action of the keys before you buy a particular laptop, to ensure that they are not too "soft", i.e. that there is enough resistance when they are pressed.

One of the main differences between a laptop and a desktop computer is the mouse (or pointing device) that controls the on-screen cursor. In the early days of laptops, some of them had a small control stick to move the cursor. However, these have almost universally been replaced by touch pads, which are small, sensitive, square or rectangular pads that are activated by stroking a finger over them to move the cursor. It sometimes takes a bit of practice to get used to them but after a little experience they can be as effective as a traditional mouse. When using a keyboard or touch pad, avoid having your fingers too high:

Instead, keep your hands and fingers as flat as possible over the keyboard and the touch pad:

Don't forget

Laptop keyboards contain the same functionality as any standard computer keyboard. However, most manufacturers have keyboards with functions that are specific to their own laptops. If this is the case the functionality will be explained in the laptop's manual.

Using an External Mouse

Not everyone likes touch pads as a means of moving the cursor on a laptop and it is true they can sometimes be slightly fiddly and prone to erratic movement if the control is too jerky. The good news is that it is perfectly possible to use a conventional mouse with a laptop to move the cursor.

A mouse can be connected to a laptop via one of the suitable sockets (ports) at the back of the laptop. These are usually in the form of USB ports:

Once the mouse has been connected to the laptop it can be used in exactly the same way as with a desktop computer. In some cases it is possible to add a wireless mouse, which can be used without the need for a cable:

Ports and Slots

Most laptops have a slightly bewildering array of sockets and slots for connecting external devices. The sockets are known as ports, and these come in a variety of shapes for different devices:

- **USB.** This is a method for connecting a variety of external devices such as digital cameras, MP3 music players, scanners and printers. The latest standard in widespread use is USB 2.0 and this has largely replaced parallel and serial ports in terms of connecting devices such as printers or an external mouse

- **FireWire.** This is a similar method of data transfer to USB but it is much faster. For this reason it is generally used for devices that need to transfer larger amounts of data, such as digital video cameras. If a laptop does not have a FireWire port, one can be added using one of the expansion slots (see below)

- **HDMI (High-Definition Multimedia Interface).** This can be used to connect to compatible digital devices, including high-definition TVs

- **Multi-card readers.** These are used for downloading photos from memory cards from digital cameras

The slots that are provided with laptops, and usually appear at the side, come in two main types:

- **CD/DVD players or re-writers.**

- **Expansion slots.** These are empty compartments that can have various types of expansion cards fitted into them to give the laptop increased functionality. These can include video cards, sound cards and wireless network cards to enable the laptop to connect to a network without the need for a cable or built-in connection

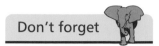
Some laptops now come equipped with USB 3.0 ports. These can still be used with USB 2.0 (or earlier) devices but they will also work with any USB 3.0 devices.

Don't forget

An expansion card is a solid board that contains circuits with the information needed for the required task. The expansion card can then communicate with the laptop's operating system.

The Wonder of Wireless

For anyone who has struggled with a tangle of computer cables and wires, the advent of wireless technology has been one of the great computer breakthroughs of recent years.

Wireless technology does exactly what the name suggests: it allows a wireless-enabled computer to communicate with other similarly-enabled devices, such as other computers, printers or an Internet connection. First of all, the devices have to be set up as a network, i.e. they have to be linked together so that they know they should be communicating with each other. Once this has been done, files can be shared or sent to the printer, and the Internet browsed, all without the need to connect the devices using a cable.

In order to be part of a wireless network, a laptop has to have a wireless capability. Most modern laptops come with wireless cards already installed; otherwise, they can be installed in any available expansion slot.

Hotspots

One of the great growth areas of wireless technology is hotspots. These are public areas that have been set up to distribute the Internet wirelessly. This means that anyone with a wireless card in their laptop can, if they are within a certain range, access the Internet in a variety of public places. These include:

- Coffee shops
- Airports
- Hotels
- Libraries
- Supermarkets

Hotspots operate using Wi-Fi technology, which is the method by which the signal from the network is transferred to individual users. Most hotspots have a limited range of approximately 100 yards. Some are free to use, while others charge a fee, depending on usage.

Beware

One concern about hotspots is security. This is because if you can access a network wirelessly, someone else could then also access your laptop and data. Many hotspots have software in place to try to stop this.

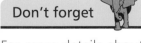

Don't forget

For more details about Wi-Fi and networks, see Chapter Nine.

Cleaning a Laptop

Like most things, laptops benefit greatly from a little care and attention. The two most important areas to keep clean are the screen and the keyboard.

Cleaning the screen

All computer screens quickly collect dust and fingerprints, and laptops are no different. If this is left too long it can make the screen harder to read and cause eye strain and headaches. Clean the screen regularly with the following cleaning materials:

- A lint-free cloth, similar to the type used to clean camera lenses (it is important not to scratch the screen in any way)

- An alcohol-free cleaning fluid that is recommended for computer screens

- Screen wipes, again that are recommended for use on computer screens

Cleaning the keyboard

Keyboards are notorious for accumulating dust, fluff and crumbs. One way to solve this problem is to turn the laptop upside down and very gently shake it to loosen any foreign objects. Failing this, a can of condensed air can be used with a narrow nozzle to blow out any stubborn items that remain lodged in the keys.

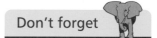

Don't forget

The outer casing of a laptop can be cleaned with the same fluid as used for the screen. Equally effective can be a duster or a damp (but not wet) cloth and warm water. Keep soap away from laptops if possible.

23

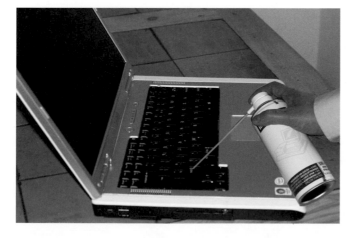

Choosing a Carry Case

When you are transporting your laptop it could be placed in any convenient bag, such as a backpack, a duffle bag or even a large handbag. However, there are several advantages to using a proper laptop carry case:

- It will probably be more comfortable when you are carrying it, as it is designed specifically for this job

- The laptop will be more secure, as it should fit properly in the case

- You should be able to keep all of your laptop accessories in one case

Beware

A laptop case should also be lockable, either with its own internal lock, or with a fastening through which a padlock can be put.

When choosing a carry case, look for one that fits your laptop well and has a strap to keep it secure inside:

Also, make sure that there are enough additional spaces and pockets for accessories, such as cables and an external mouse. Finally, choosing a case with a padded shoulder strap will be of considerable benefit if you have to carry your laptop for any length of time.

Spares and Accessories

Whenever you are going anywhere with your laptop there are always spares and accessories to consider. Some of these are just nice things to have, while others could be essential to ensure that you can still use your laptop if anything goes wrong while you are on your travels. Items to consider for putting in your laptop case include:

- **Spare battery.** This is probably the most important spare if you are going to be away from home for any length of time, and particularly if you think you may be unable to access a power supply for a period of time, and so be unable to charge your laptop battery. Like all batteries, laptop batteries slowly lose power over time and do not keep their charge for as long as when they are new. It is a good idea to always keep an eye on how much battery power you have left and, if you are running low, to try and conserve as much energy as possible. Although laptop batteries are bulky and heavy, carrying a spare could mean the difference between frustration and relief, if you are left with no battery power

- **Power cable.** This is the cable that can be used to power the laptop when it is not being run on battery power. It usually consists of a cable and a power adapter, which makes it rather bulky and heavy. Whenever possible this should be used rather than the internal battery, and it should be kept with the laptop at all times

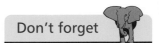

Don't forget

For more information on batteries see Chapter 10.

...cont'd

Hot tip

It is important that headphones are comfortable to wear for an extended period of time. In general, the types that fit over the ears are more comfortable than the "bud" variety that are inserted into the ear.

Don't forget

Backing up is the process of copying folders and files from your laptop onto an external device for safekeeping in case the folders and files on the laptop are deleted or corrupted.

- **External mouse.** This can be used instead of the laptop's touch pad or track ball. Some people prefer a traditional mouse, particularly if they are going to be working on their laptop for an extended period of time

- **Multi-card reader.** If you do not have a built-in multi-card reader (see page 21) an external one can be used to download photos from a digital camera memory card. This will connect via a USB port

- **Headphones.** These can be used to listen to music or films if you are in the company of other people and you do not want to disturb them. They can also be very useful if there are distracting noises from other people

- **Pen drive.** This is a small device that can be used to copy data to and from your laptop. It connects via a USB port and is about the size of a packet of chewing gum. It is an excellent way of backing up files from your laptop when you are away from home

- **Cleaning material.** The materials described on page 23 can be taken to ensure your laptop is always in tip-top condition for use

- **DVDs/CDs.** Video or music DVDs and CDs can be taken to provide mobile entertainment, and blank ones can be taken to copy data onto, similar to using a pen drive

2 Around a Laptop

This chapter shows how to quickly become familiar with your laptop, and the new Windows 8 operating system, so that you can start to use it productively. It covers starting the laptop and gives an overview of Windows 8 so that you can become comfortable with this new environment. It also looks at accessing old favorites such as the Desktop and the Control Panel.

Opening Up and Turning On

The first step towards getting started with a new laptop is to open it ready for use. The traditional clamshell design keeps the screen and keyboard together through the use of an internal clip or connector. This can be released by a button on the exterior of the laptop, which is usually positioned at the front or side. Some laptops have a magnetic connection between the screen and the main body.

Once the screen has been opened it can then be positioned ready for use. The screen should stay in any position in which it is placed:

The power button for turning on a laptop, ready for use, is usually located near to the keyboard:

The laptop can be turned on by pushing this button firmly. The laptop will then probably make a chime, to indicate that it has been turned on, and begin loading the operating system (the software that is used to run and manage all of the laptop's apps, folders and files). Once the laptop has completed its startup procedure the opening screen should be displayed. At this point the laptop is ready for use.

Touch Screen Laptops

Windows 8 is the latest operating system from Microsoft and this will be installed on new laptops. It is optimized for touch screen use, so it is ideal for using with laptops with touch screen capability and also with Windows 8 tablets.

Touch screen laptops still have a traditional keyboard but navigation can also be done by tapping, swiping and pinching on the screen. Some of the functions that can be performed on a touch screen laptop are:

- Activate a button, such as Done or OK, by tapping on it. Apps on the new Windows 8 interface can also be accessed by tapping on them on the Start screen

- Move up and down long pages by swiping in the required direction, e.g. to navigate around web pages. The Charms bar within the Windows 8 interface can also be accessed by swiping inwards from the right-hand side

- Zoom in and out of pages by pinching inwards, or outwards, with thumb and forefinger (if the open app has this functionality). It is most commonly used for zooming in and out of web pages

Most leading laptop manufacturers now have a range of touch screen laptops; some to look at include:

- The Acer Iconia
- Dell's XPS Duo 12
- HP's Envy TouchSmart and Spectre
- Sony's VAIO T13
- Toshiba's Satellite U925t

The current range of touch screen laptops tends to be more in the netbook range in terms of screen size. However, as the technology develops, more and more laptops will have this functionality. Also, a number of touch screen models can also be converted into tablet mode, either by revolving the screen, or sliding it over the keyboard.

Don't forget

See page 39 for details about navigating with touch in Windows 8.

Windows 8 Interface

Windows 8 is the most significant change to the Windows operating system since Windows 95 helped redefine the way that we look at personal computers. The most obvious change in Windows 8 is the new Windows 8 interface. This will be the first view of Windows 8 and all of the elements are accessed through the brightly-colored Start screen.

The Windows 8 interface defines one of the main purposes of Windows 8: it is an operating system designed for the mobile generation so it is ideal for use on a laptop. It also operates on desktops, tablets and cell phones, so it's possible to synchronize Windows 8 so that all of your settings and apps will be available over multiple devices through an online Microsoft Account.

Don't forget

Windows 8 apps are designed to be used in full-screen mode and cannot be minimized in the traditional way with Windows programs.

30

Another innovation in Windows 8 is the greater use of custom apps (applications) that are accessed from the Start screen. This is done through the colored tiles: each tile gives access to the relevant app. For instance, if you

click or tap on the Photos app you will be able to view, organize and edit your photo files and folders. A lot of the Windows 8 apps are linked together too, so it is easy to share content through your apps.

There are also a number of Windows 8 Charms that can be accessed at any point within Windows 8 to give a range of functionality. These can be accessed from the right-hand side of the screen.

Don't forget

For a detailed look at working with the Windows 8 Charms, see Chapter Three.

Even though Windows 8 has a very modern look with the Windows 8 interface, old favorites such as the Desktop are not far away. The Desktop and all of its functionality that users have got used to with previous versions of Windows is available at the click or tap of a button and this takes you into an environment that, initially, may be more familiar.

In a way, Windows 8 can be thought of as two operating systems that have been merged: the new Windows 8 interface, with its reliance on apps; and the traditional Windows one, with access to items through the Desktop.

It can take a bit of time getting used to working with the two interfaces.

The Start Screen

The first, and most obvious, difference about Windows 8 over previous versions of Windows, is that the Start Button is no more. This was the button in the bottom left-hand corner of the screen from which programs and various areas of the computer were accessed. In Windows 8 this has been replaced by the Start screen, which is part of the new Windows 8 interface.

The Start screen is a collection of large, brightly colored, tiles. By default these are the apps (programs) which are provided with Windows 8. At first sight, the Start screen is a big change from previous Windows' interfaces. But don't panic: there is considerable functionality on the Start screen for finding items, getting around and customizing Windows 8. Also, it is still possible to access your old Windows favorites such as the Desktop and the Control Panel.

Don't forget

It may take a bit of time to get used to the new Start screen compared to previous versions of Windows. However, the more you use it the more you will begin to use the potential of this ground-breaking version of Windows.

The Windows 8 apps are shown as colored tiles. These are the built-in apps that have been designed specifically for use with Windows 8. Much of the functionality of the Start screen works best with these apps.

Another change in Windows 8 is that there are no scroll bars visible on the Start screen. However, they are still there and can be used to view the rest of the Start screen:

1 Move the cursor over the bottom of the screen to access the scroll bar and scroll to the right to view all of the apps on the Start screen

When you are working in any app, the Start screen can be accessed at any time by moving the cursor over the bottom left-hand corner of the screen. When the Start screen icon appears, click or tap on it to move to the Start screen.

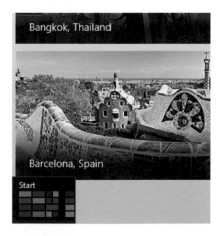

The Desktop

One of the first things you may say when you initially see Windows 8 is, "Where is the Desktop?". This is a fair question, given that the first thing you will see is the multi-colored Start screen. But the Desktop has not been removed: it is just sitting behind the Start screen. To access it:

1 On the Start screen, click or tap on the **Desktop** tile

2 By default, the Taskbar at the bottom of the Desktop contains icons for Internet Explorer and File Explorer

3 Move the cursor over items on the Taskbar to see tooltips about the item. When apps are opened their icons appear on the Taskbar

4 The notifications area at the right-hand side of the Taskbar has speaker, network and other system tools. Click or tap on one to see more information about each item

The Control Panel

The Control Panel is a popular and valuable feature of Windows, but it may not be immediately obvious how to access it in Windows 8. There are a couple of ways to do this:

1. On the Start screen, right-click and click or tap on the **All apps** button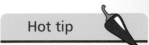

2. Scroll to the right and click or tap on the **Control Panel** button,

or

1. Right-click over the bottom left-hand corner of the screen and click or tap on the **Control Panel** link

Task Manager
Control Panel
Windows Explorer
Search
Run
Desktop

2. Click or tap on the sections within the Control Panel to see more options for each and apply settings

Hot tip

The Control Panel can also be accessed by selecting the Settings Charm when in the Desktop interface and selecting **Control Panel** from under Settings.

35

Hot tip

The Control Panel can be pinned to the Desktop Taskbar for quick access. To do this, select **All apps** on the Start screen. Right-click on the **Control Panel** button and select **Pin to taskbar** from the toolbar at the bottom of the screen. This is also a good option for other apps too.

Navigating Windows 8

Since Windows 8 is optimized for use with touch screen devices this introduces a new factor when it comes to navigating around the system, particularly the new Windows 8 interface. The three ways of doing this are:

- Mouse

- Keyboard

- Touch

Some of these methods can be used in conjunction with each other (for instance mouse and keyboard, and touch and keyboard) but the main ways of getting around Windows 8 with each are:

Mouse

- Move the mouse to the bottom left-hand corner to access the Start screen. Click on it once when it appears. This can be done from any app or the Desktop

- Move the cursor over the top or bottom right-hand corners to access the Charms bar. Move down and click on one to access it

Don't forget

One of the most obvious changes on the Start screen is how to turn off or restart your Windows 8 laptop. For details see page 42.

- Move the cursor over the top left-hand corner to view the most recently-used app. Click on it to access it

- Move the cursor over the top left-hand corner and drag down the left-hand side to view all of the currently-open apps (App Switcher). Click on one to access it

- In an open Windows 8 app, right-click to access the bottom toolbar. This will have options specific to the app in use

- In an open Windows 8 app, click and hold at the top of the window and drag down to the bottom of the screen to close the app

...cont'd

Keyboard

The majority of the keyboard shortcuts for navigating around Windows 8 are accessed in conjunction with the WinKey. Press:

- **WinKey** to access the Start screen at any time

- **WinKey** + **L** to lock the computer and display the Lock screen

- **WinKey** + **C** to access the Charms bar

- **WinKey** + **I** to access the Settings Charm

- **WinKey** + **K** to access the Devices Charm

- **WinKey** + **H** to access the Share Charm

- **WinKey** + **Q** to access the Search Charm to search over apps

- **WinKey** + **F** to access the Search Charm to search over files

- **WinKey** + **D** to access the Desktop

- **WinKey** + **M** to access the Desktop with the active window minimized

- **WinKey** + **E** to access File Explorer, displaying the Computer folder

- **WinKey** + **T** to display the thumbnails on the Desktop Taskbar

- **WinKey** + **U** to access the Ease of Access Center

- **WinKey** + **X** to access administration tools and quick access to items including the Desktop and the Control Panel

- **WinKey** + **Z** in a Windows 8 app to display the app's toolbar at the bottom of the screen

- **Alt** + **F4** to close a Windows 8 app

Touch

To navigate around Windows 8 with a touch screen laptop:

- Tap on an item to access it

- Swipe inwards from the right-hand edge to access the Charms bar

- Swipe inwards from the left-hand edge to switch between currently-open apps

- Swipe inwards slowly from the left-hand edge and drag one of the apps away from the App Switcher to snap it to the left-hand side

- Swipe inwards from the left and then back again to show the currently-open apps (App Switcher)

- In an open Windows 8 app, swipe upwards from the bottom of the screen, or downwards from the top of the screen, to access the app's toolbar

- In an open Windows 8 app, swipe down from inside the app to view its settings

- In an open Windows 8 app, hold at the top of the screen and drag down to the bottom to close the app

- On the Start screen, swipe down on an app's tile to view additional options relating to the app

- Pinch outwards to minimize the Start screen. Pinch inwards to return to normal view

Hot tip

To perform a right-click operation on a Windows 8 touch screen laptop, tap and hold on an item on the screen until a contextual menu appears. This will contain the options that you can perform for the selected item.

Don't forget

For a touch screen laptop, swipe left or right to move through the Start screen.

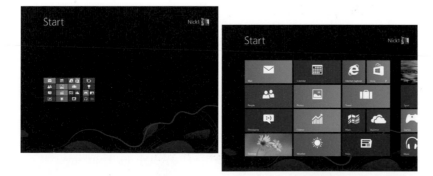

Using a Microsoft Account

We live in a world of ever-increasing computer connectivity, where users expect to be able to access their content wherever they are and share it with their friends and family in a variety of ways. This is known as cloud computing, with content being stored on online servers, from where it can be accessed by authorized users.

In Window 8 this type of connectivity is achieved with a Microsoft Account. This is a registration system that can be set up with most email addresses and a password, and provides access to a number of services via the Windows 8 apps. These include:

- **Mail.** This is the Windows 8 email app that can be used to access and manage your different email accounts

- **Messaging.** This is the text messaging app

- **People.** This is the address book app

- **Calendar.** This is the calendar and organizer app

- **The Windows Store.** This is the online store for previewing and downloading additional apps

- **SkyDrive.** This is the online sharing (cloud computing) service

Creating a Microsoft Account
It is free to create a Microsoft Account and this provides a unique identifier for logging into your Microsoft Account and the related apps. There are several ways in which you can create a Microsoft Account:

- During the initial setup process for Windows 8. You will be asked if you want to create a Microsoft Account at this point. If you do not, you can always do so later

- When you first open an app that requires access to a Microsoft Account. When you do this you will be prompted to create a new account

- From the Users section of the PC settings that are accessed from the Settings Charm

Don't forget

The Microsoft Account, and related services, replaces the Windows Live function. However, there will still be remnants of this online for some time and login details for this can be used for the Microsoft Account services.

Beware

Without a Windows Account you will not be able to access the full functionality of the apps listed here.

Hot tip

Microsoft Account details can also be used as your sign-in for Windows 8.

Whichever way you use to create a Microsoft Account the process is similar:

1 When you are first prompted to Sign in with a Microsoft Account, click or tap on the **Sign up for a Microsoft account** link

2 Enter an email address and a password

3 Click or tap on the **Next** button to move through the process

Next

4 Enter additional information including your name, location and zip/post code. On the next screen you also need to enter a phone number, which is used as a security measure by Microsoft if you forget your password

5 Click or tap on the **Finish** button to complete setting up your Microsoft Account

Don't forget

If you create a Microsoft Account when accessing a related app, the sign-up process will take you to the online Account Live web page, but the process is similar. In both cases you will be able to log in to the Account Live web page too, at https://login.live.com. You can also access your account details at https://account.live.com

Turning Off

It may not be immediately obvious how to shut down your laptop in Windows 8, but it can be done as follows:

1 Move the cursor over the bottom right-hand corner of the screen (this can be done from either the Windows 8 interface or the Desktop, so the computer can be shut down from both environments)

2 Click or tap on the **Settings Charm**

3 Click or tap on the **Power** button

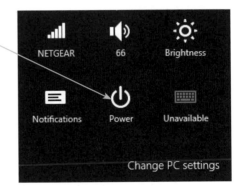

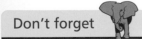
4 Click or tap on the **Shut down** or **Restart** options

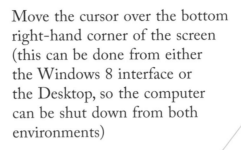

Help and Support Center

Help is at hand for Windows 8 through the Help and Support Center and also online resources:

1 Move the cursor over the bottom right-hand corner of the screen and click or tap on the **Settings Charm**

2 Click or tap on the **Help** link under the Settings heading

Settings

Start

Tiles

Help

3 If the Help link is accessed in this way from the Start screen, this Help window is available. This takes you to online Help pages

← Help

Adding apps, websites, and more to Start

Finding things with Search

Rearranging tiles on Start

Need more help?

Learn the basics:
Get started with Windows 8 and Start

Get support:
Visit the Windows website

4 If the Help link is accessed in this way from the Desktop, this Help window is available

Don't forget

Enter keywords into the Search box in Step 4 to look for specific help items.

5 Click or tap on a link to view additional information about specific topics

Screen Resolution

If you have a high resolution screen, you may find that the text as well as the icons are too small. You can increase the effective size by reducing the screen resolution.

 Access the Control Panel and select **Appearance and Personalization** and select **Adjust screen resolution**

2 Click or tap the down arrow next to **Resolution**

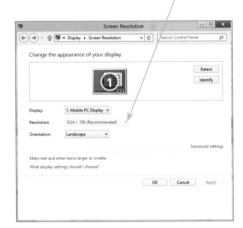

3 Drag the slider, then click or tap **Apply**

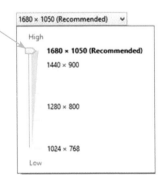

4 Click or tap the down arrow next to Orientation to switch the view to **Portrait**

Adjusting Text

As well as changing the overall screen resolution, it is also possible to adjust the size at which text is displayed on the screen. To do this:

 Access the Control Panel and select **Appearance and Personalization** and then select **Display**

Display
Make text and other items larger or smaller
Adjust screen resolution

2. Select, for example, **Medium – 125%**, and select **Apply**

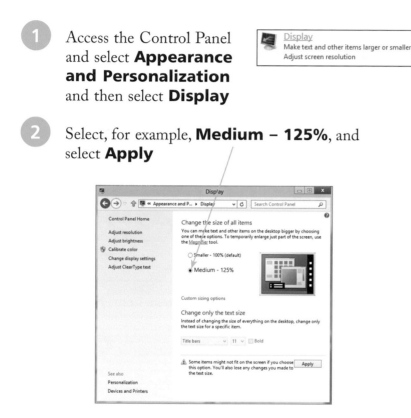

Don't forget

You can change your display settings and make it easier to read what is on the screen.

45

3. Sign out and log back in to apply the change

Microsoft Windows

You must sign out of your computer to apply these changes

Save any open files and close all programs before you sign out.

Sign out now   Sign out later

4. Everything on the screen is increased in size if the display size is increased

Adjusting Volume

There are different sources of sounds on a laptop. The main two are:

- Sounds from the speakers
- System Windows sounds

The volume for each of these can be adjusted independently of the other. To do this:

1 Access the Control Panel and click or tap on the **Hardware and Sound** link

Hardware and Sound
View devices and printers
Add a device
Adjust commonly used mobility settings

2 In the Sound section, click on the **Adjust system volume** link

Sound
Adjust system volume
Change system sounds
Manage audio devices

3 In the Volume Mixer window, drag the sliders to adjust the volume for a particular item

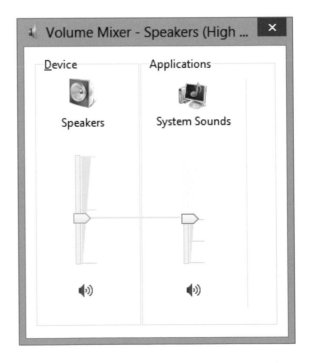

Loading CDs and DVDs

CDs and DVDs are an important aspect of life with a laptop. They can be used to store information and also for playing music or movies, particularly when traveling. To load CDs or DVDs:

1 Locate the CD or DVD drive. This will be a slot that is located at the side or front of the laptop

2 Press the button on the front of the drive once to eject the tray

3 Insert the CD or DVD into the tray and press the button again to close it, or push it in gently

4 To view the location of the CD or DVD, click or tap the **Computer** button in the File Explorer. The CD or DVD will be shown as a separate drive

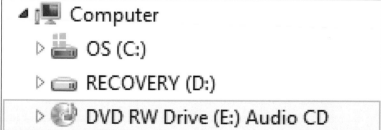

Beware

By default, movie DVDs cannot be played on Windows 8 laptops. To do this you have to download and buy an enhanced version of the Windows Media Player from the Microsoft website.

Don't forget

For more details about using music and videos on your laptop, see Chapter Six.

Adding Devices

In most cases Windows will automatically install the software that will allow devices to work on your computer. However, on occasions you may have to do this manually, e.g. if you want to add a new printer to your PC. This can be done through the Hardware and Sound section in the Control Panel and the PC settings.

1 Connect the printer to the computer, either with a cable or wirelessly, and switch the printer on

2 Open the Control Panel and click or tap on the **View devices and printers** link under the Hardware and Sound heading

3 Click or tap on the **Add a printer** link at the top of the Devices and Printers window

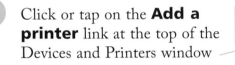

4 Select the printer that you want to add and click or tap on the **Next** button

5 Select a driver for the printer and click or tap on the **Next** button

6 Select a name for the printer as required. This is what will appear when you select to print an item

7   If you would like other computers on the network to share the printer, click or tap on this button

8   Click or tap on the **Print a test page** button and click on the **Finish** button to complete adding the printer

Adding devices through PC settings

Devices such as printers can also be added through the PC settings of the Setting Charm.

1   Access the Settings Charm and click or tap on the **Change PC settings** button

Change PC settings

2   Click or tap on the **Devices** button

Devices

3   Click or tap on the **Add a device** button

Devices

+ Add a device

Dell Laser Printer 1720

4   To delete a device, click or tap on it in the Devices section and click or tap on this button

Dell Laser Printer 1720dn
Offline

5   Click or tap on the **Remove** button

Are you sure you want to remove this device?

Remove

Pen Drives

Pen drives are small devices that can be used for copying files and then transferring them between computers. In some ways they are the natural successor to floppy discs. To connect a pen drive to a laptop and use it:

Hot tip

Because of their size, pen drives can be lost quite easily. When traveling, attach them to something like a keyring or keep them in a small pocket in your laptop case.

1 Connect the pen drive to one of the laptop's USB ports

2 The pen drive should be recognized automatically and the necessary software installed so that it is ready to use

3 Access the Desktop and click or tap on the **File Explorer** button on the Taskbar

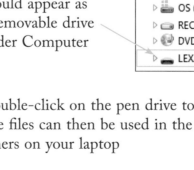

Hot tip

The File Explorer can also be accessed from the **All apps** option from the Start screen. See page 83 for details about accessing All apps.

4 The pen drive should appear as a removable drive under Computer

5 Double-click on the pen drive to view its contents. The files can then be used in the same way as any others on your laptop

3 Getting Up and Running

This chapter looks further into Windows 8, focusing on the new Start screen and personalizing the way it looks. It also shows how to access the File Explorer and use it to organize your files and folders.

Sign-in Options

Each time you start up your computer you will need to sign in. This is a security feature so that no-one else can gain unauthorized access to your account on your PC. This sign-in process starts with the Lock screen and then you have to enter your login password.

1 When you start your PC the Lock screen will be showing. This can only be opened by your password

2 Click or tap on the **Lock screen**, or press any key, to move to the login screen. Enter your password and press **Enter** or click or tap on this arrow

3 On the login screen, click or tap on this button to select Ease of Access options

4 Click or tap on this button to select Power off options including Shut Down and Restart

5 On the login screen, click or tap on this button to view the login screen for all users on the PC

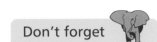
Don't forget

6 Click or tap on another user to access their own login screen

53

Login settings

Settings for how you log in can be accessed from the Users section in the PC settings:

1 Access the PC settings and click or tap on the **Users** button

PC settings

Personalize

Users

2 Select options to change your password, create a picture password or create a PIN instead of a password

Sign-in options

Change your password

Create a picture password

Create a PIN

Don't forget

For details about accessing and using PC settings see pages 60–65.

3 If you want to create a picture password you must have a touch screen device. Select a picture and draw a pattern to use as your login

Welcome to picture password

Picture password is a new way to help you protect your touchscreen PC. You choose the picture — and the gestures you use with it — to create a password that's uniquely yours.

When you've chosen a picture, you "draw" directly on the touchscreen to create a combination of circles, straight lines, and taps. The size, position, and direction of your gestures become part of your picture password.

Choose picture

Charms

As shown in Chapter Two, the Charms can be accessed by moving the cursor over the bottom or top right-hand corners of the screen. The Charms are, from top to bottom:

- Search
- Share
- Start screen
- Devices
- Settings

The Charms can be accessed at anytime, from any app, by moving the cursor over the bottom or top right-hand corners of the screen. Therefore if you want to access, for instance, the Start screen while you are working in the Photos app this can be done with the Start screen Charm.

Settings

The Settings Charm can be used to access the Start screen Settings and also PC settings for personalizing the Start screen (see page 62 for more details). It can also be accessed from any app and used for settings for that specific app. So, if you are working in the Mail app and select the Settings Charm, you will be provided with the Mail Settings. Or, if you are in Internet Explorer you will be provided with settings for this and so on. To use the Settings Charm:

Don't forget

When you access the Charms bar, a separate panel displays the date, time, Wi-Fi connection and battery charge level.

1. Access the Charms and click or tap on the **Settings Charm**

2. At the bottom of the panel are the default settings that are always available from the Settings Charm

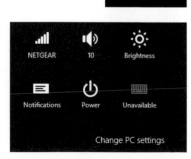

NETGEAR 10 Brightness

Notifications Power Unavailable

Change PC settings

3 At the top of the panel are settings specific to the Start screen

4 Open an app and select the **Settings Charm**. The default settings are still available at the bottom of the panel, but the top now has settings options for the active app, i.e. the one currently being used. For example, these are the settings for Internet Explorer 10

Devices

The Devices Charm can be used to send items in an app to any available device. For instance, if you are viewing a photo in the Photos app, you can use the Devices Charm to send it to any available printers. To use the Devices Charm:

1 Access the Charms and click or tap on the **Devices Charm**

2 Select a Device. The related task will then be undertaken, i.e. an item will be sent to a printer

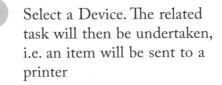

Beware

The Devices Charm only works from compatible devices on the Start screen, but not the Desktop. For instance, the Photos app will usually have printer devices available, but if you open a word processing app, such as Word, on the Desktop then there will be no devices available from the Devices Charm. However, items such as printers can still be accessed from the app's Menu bar on the Desktop as in previous versions of Windows.

...cont'd

Start screen Charm

Click or tap on this Charm to return to the Start screen at any point from within Windows 8.

Share Charm

The Share Charm can be used to share items within an app with the suite of apps including Mail and People (the address book app). To use the Share Charm:

1 Access the Charms and click or tap on the **Share Charm**

2 Select the app with which you want to share the current content. This could involve emailing a photo to someone or sending a web page directly to a contact in the People app

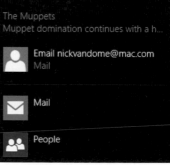

Don't forget

To use the Share Charm you have to first select an item in an appropriate app, i.e. select a photo in the Photos app and then access the Charm.

Search Charm

The Search Charm can be used to search for items within the app in which you are working. For instance, if the Video app is open then the search will be conducted over this by default.

The Search Charm can also be used to search over your computer and your apps. To use the Search Charm:

 Access the Charms and click on the **Search Charm**

 Select an area over which you want to perform the search, e.g. Settings in this case

 When working in an app, select the **Search Charm**. This can be used to automatically search over the app which you are currently using

Charm Shortcuts

The individual Charms can also be accessed with keyboard shortcuts. These are:

- All Charms: **WinKey + C**
- Settings Charm: **WinKey + I**
- Devices Charm: **WinKey + K**
- Start screen: **WinKey**
- Sharing Charm: **WinKey + H**
- Search Charm: **WinKey + Q**

When you enter search words into the Search box, suggestions appear below, relating to the app over which you are performing the search.

Don't forget

The WinKey is the one with the Windows icon on the keyboard.

Default Settings

As shown on page 54 some of the settings on the Settings Charm are available whenever this is accessed, regardless of which app you are in. To use these:

1 Access the Settings Charm by moving the cursor over the bottom or top right-hand corners and click or tap on this icon

2 The default settings appear at the bottom of the panel, above the Change PC settings link

3 Click or tap on this button to access Network and Wi-Fi settings

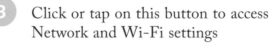

4 If you have moved to a level down in the Settings structure, click or tap on this button at the top of the panel to move back one level

5 Click or tap on this button to adjust the volume. Drag this slider to make the adjustment

6 Click or tap on this button to adjust the screen brightness. Drag this slider to make the adjustment

Brightness

Don't forget

Notifications can be set for a variety of apps so that you are alerted when there is new information. Settings for notifications can be selected within the Notifications section of the PC settings.

7 Click or tap on this button to specify timescales for when notifications appear

Notifications

Hide for 8 hours

Hide for 3 hours

Hide for 1 hour

8 Click or tap on this button to access options for shutting down and restarting the computer

Power

9 If a virtual keyboard is available, click or tap on this button to access its settings

Unavailable

Personalize Settings

The Settings Charm enables you to set the appearance of the Lock screen, the Start screen and select an account photo. To do this first access the PC settings:

1 Access the Charms and click or tap on the **Settings Charm**

2 Click or tap on the **Change PC settings** link

3 Click or tap on the **Personalize** button underneath the PC settings heading

Personalizing the Lock screen

To personalize the Lock screen:

1 Click or tap on the **Lock screen** link at the top of the Personalize page

2 Click or tap on one of the thumbnail images to select a new image for the Lock screen

60

3 The selected image becomes the Lock screen background

 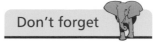
4 Click or tap on the **Browse** button to select an image from your hard drive for the Lock screen background

5 Select an image and click or tap on **Choose picture** to set the image as the Lock screen background

6 The image is added as the background for the Lock screen

...cont'd

Personalizing the Start screen

There are also settings for the appearance of the Start screen:

1. Click or tap on the **Start screen** link at the top of the Personalize page

2. The settings enable you to change the background color and pattern

3. Click or tap on one of these thumbnails to select a background pattern

Don't forget

The color schemes for the background, i.e. the different shades, are preset for each color and cannot be changed.

4. Drag this slider to select a background color

5. The selections in Steps 3 and 4 are applied to the Start screen background

Personalizing the Account Photo

To set your own photo for your personal account:

1 Click or tap on the **Account picture** link at the top of the Personalize page

2 Click or tap on the **Browse** button to select a picture for your account

3 Select a photo or picture and click or tap on the **Choose picture** button to add it as your account picture

4 The photo is displayed on the Personalize screen

5 The photo is also displayed at the top right-hand corner of the Start screen where you can lock the screen or change users

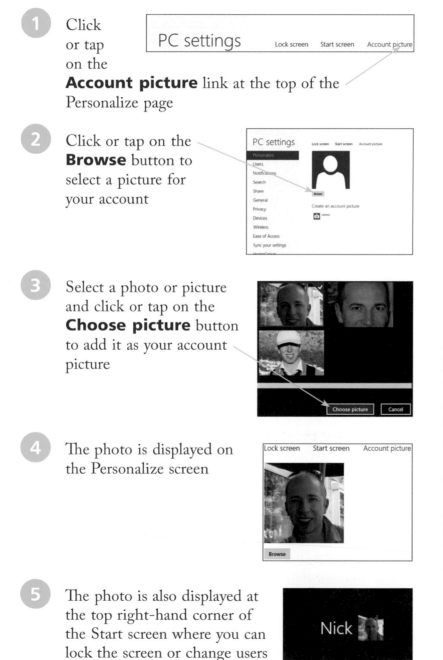

Hot tip

The Account picture can also be changed by selecting your account name at the top right-hand corner of the screen and selecting the **Change account picture** link. This takes you to the Personalize screen at Step 2 here.

63

Users settings

Select the **Users** button to select options for switching accounts, changing your password and adding more users.

Don't forget

The Users settings can be used to switch between a Microsoft Account and a local account for signing in to your laptop.

PC settings

Personalize
Users
Notifications
Search
Share
General
Privacy
Devices
Wireless
Ease of Access
Sync your settings
HomeGroup

Your account

Nick Vandome
nickvandome@gmail.com

Your saved passwords for apps, websites, and networks won't sync until you trust this PC. Trust this PC.

You can switch to a local account, but your settings won't sync between the PCs you use.

Switch to a local account

More account settings online

Sign-in options

Change your password

Create a picture password

Create a PIN

Any user who has a password doesn't need to enter it when waking this PC.

Change

Other users

Notifications settings

Select the **Notifications** button to select options for the apps for which you will receive notifications. These will appear on the app tiles and some will also appear in pop-up boxes on the Start screen. They include new emails and messages and updated news items. Drag these buttons to turn the notifications On or Off.

Search settings

Select the **Search** button to select which apps you would like to use for searching items over. For instance, using search over the Internet Explorer app means that you will be able to search over the web with this function.

Share settings

Select the **Share** button to select options for how content is shared between apps. If the apps for sharing are turned Off then you will not be able to share content, such as photos, with these apps.

General settings

Select the **General** button to select options for the location of the time for your PC, allowing switching between apps, Autocorrect for misspelled words, the language for input devices, refreshing your whole PC for improved performance, reinstalling Windows and the Advanced startup.

Privacy settings

Select the **Privacy** button to select options for letting apps use your geographical location over the Internet and also let them access your account username and picture. There is also an option for sending information to the Windows Store about the web content that your apps use.

Devices settings

Select the **Devices** button to add new devices such as printers. Click or tap on the Add a device button to start the process (see pages 48–49 for more details).

Wireless settings

Select the **Wireless** button to select options for Airplane mode to stop wireless communications and to turn Wi-Fi on your computer On or Off.

Ease of Access settings

Select the **Ease of Access** button to select options for making the PC easier to use for people with visual or mobility issues. This includes the contrast of the screen, the size of everything on the screen (images and text) and options for turning On the Magnifier, Narrator and On-Screen Keyboard.

Sync your settings

Select the **Sync your settings** button to select options for syncing items that can then be used when you access your Microsoft Account from another online device.

HomeGroup settings

Select the **HomeGroup** button to select options for creating a HomeGroup for sharing your files with another Windows 8 PC. In this section there is a codeword that can be entered into the other PC to access your HomeGroup. (See Chapter Nine for more details about HomeGroups.)

Windows Update settings

Select the **Windows Update** button to select options for how your PC handles updates to Windows 8. By default, they are set to be installed automatically.

Don't forget

Devices should be switched on and connected to your laptop or network for them to be found and then added.

Hot tip

The Ease of Access options can also be accessed from: the login screen by pressing **WinKey + U**. Use the Ease of Access Magnifier option to increase the size of items underneath the magnifying glass icon that can be moved around to magnify different parts of the screen.
Use the Ease of Access Narrator to activate the speech function whereby the items on the screen will be read aloud to you.

Beware

Sync settings can only be changed if you are logged in with a Microsoft Account.

Organizing the Start Screen

By default, the new Windows 8 apps are organized into two groups on the Start screen. These are mainly the communication and information apps in the left-hand group and the entertainment apps in the right-hand group. However, it is possible to fully-customize the way that the apps are organized on the Start screen. To do this:

1 Move the cursor over the bottom right-hand corner and click or tap on this button to minimize the groups on the Start screen

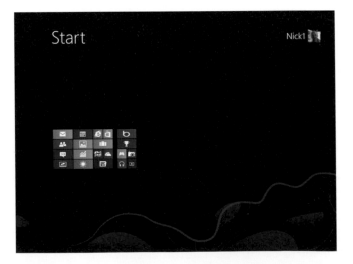

2 Right-click on a group to select it. A tick will appear in the top right-hand corner to indicate the group is selected

3 Drag the group to move its position on the Start screen

Moving tiles

Tiles can be rearranged within their respective groups. To do this:

1 Click, or press, and hold on a tile and drag it into a new position in the group

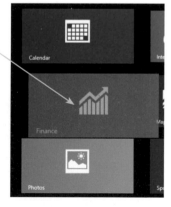

2 The other tiles move to accommodate the tile in its new position

...cont'd

Creating new groups

The two default groups of apps can be expanded by creating new groups from the existing ones. This is done by dragging the app tiles out of their current groups to create new ones. To do this:

1 Click, or tap, and hold on a tile and drag it away from its current group until a thick vertical line appears behind the tile

2 Drag the tile into its new position to create a new group

Resizing tiles

As well as rearranging tiles, their sizes can also be edited on the Start screen. Initially the tiles are a mixture of small and large sizes. However, the size of each tile can be changed. To do this:

1 Right-click on a tile to select it and click or tap on the **Smaller** button on the toolbar at the bottom of the screen

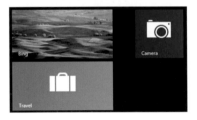

2 The tile is resized. If the tiles next to it are all larger then a space will appear next to the resized tile

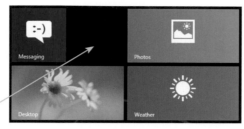

3 To enlarge a tile, right-click on it and click on the **Larger** button. If there is a space next to it, the resized tile will fill it. If there is no space then the other tiles will move to accommodate the new, larger, tile

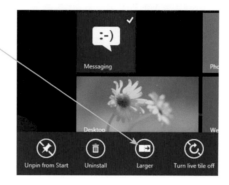

Don't forget

From a design point of view it is a good idea to have a mixture of larger and smaller tiles on the Start screen.

4 If there are only smaller tiles after a larger tile, these will fill the space if the larger tile is made smaller as in Step 1

5 When the larger tile is reduced in size the next tile below it moves up automatically to fill in the space

Naming Groups

In their initial state, groups on the Start screen are not named, but it is possible to give them all their own individual names or titles. To do this:

 Minimize the Start screen by moving the cursor over the bottom right-hand corner and clicking or tapping on this button

 Right-click on a group so that a tick appears on it

 Click or tap on the **Name group** button

Enter a name for the group and click or tap on the **Name** button

The name is applied at the top of the group

Snapping

Although Windows 8 apps cannot be minimized in the traditional way as with previous versions of Windows, there is a function that enables them to be 'snapped' to the left or the right of the screen so that they are available when you are working in other apps. This takes effect in both the Windows 8 interface and the Desktop environment. To snap apps in this way:

1 Move the cursor over the top left-hand corner of the screen and drag down to view the currently-open apps (in the App Switcher)

2 Click, or press, and hold on an app and drag it towards the main screen until a solid vertical bar appears (or swipe inwards slowly from the left-hand edge and drag one of the apps away from the App Switcher to snap it to the left-hand side)

3 Release the app and it will be snapped to the left-hand side of the screen

Beware

The snapping feature only works with a screen resolution of 1366 x 768 or above.

Don't forget

Click or tap on the thick border at the side of the snapped app to minimize this to a single bar. Click or tap on it again to maximize it.

71

Hot tip

To snap an app to the right-hand side, drag it across the screen to the right-hand border.

Opening File Explorer

Although File Explorer (formerly called Windows Explorer) is not necessarily one of the first apps that you will use with Windows 8 (those from the new Windows 8 interface are more likely to be examined first) it still plays an important role in organizing your folders and files. To access File Explorer:

1 Right-click on the **Start** screen and click or tap on the **All apps** button. Select the **File Explorer** button, or

2 From the Desktop, click or tap on this icon on the Taskbar, or

3 Press the **WinKey + E** combination, and File Explorer opens with the Computer folder

4 When File Explorer is opened, the current Libraries are displayed

Hot tip

You can right-click on the bottom left-hand corner of the screen, either from the Start screen or the Desktop, and access File Explorer from here.

The Taskbar

The Taskbar is permanently visible at the bottom of the screen when working in the Desktop environment.
To illustrate the range of functions that it supports:

1 Open items are displayed on the Taskbar at the bottom of the window

2 Windows of the same type will be grouped under a task button

3 Move the mouse pointer over the File Explorer shortcut to see previews of the folder windows that File Explorer is managing

4 Move the mouse pointer over the other multiple Task button to see the customization and control windows, e.g. for the Control Panel here

Since these tasks all use File Explorer, the techniques you learn when you open Computer, for example, will apply also in Documents or Pictures.

Hot tip

When you right-click the Desktop, you will find customization functions, Screen Resolution and Personalize on the displayed menu.

73

Don't forget

To see what type of app any Task button represents, right-click on it.

Scenic Ribbon

The navigation and functionality in the Libraries is done by the Scenic Ribbon at the top of the window. This has options for the Library itself and also the type of content that is being viewed:

1 Click or tap on the tabs at the top of the Library window to view associated tools

2 Click or tap on the Library Tools tab to view the menus for the whole Library (see below)

3 Click or tap on the content tab (Picture Tools in this example) to view menus for the selected content

Library File Menu
This contains options for opening a new window, closing the current window or moving to a frequently-visited location in the Library.

Library Home Menu
This contains options for copying and pasting, moving, deleting and renaming selected items. You can also create new folders, view folder properties and select folder items.

Library Share Menu

This contains options for sharing selected items, by sending them to the HomeGroup or another user on the computer, burning them to a CD or DVD, creating a compressed Zip file or sending the items to a printer.

Library View Menu

This contains options for how you view the items in the current active folder.

Library Manage Menu

This contains options for managing specific libraries. Click or tap on the Manage library button to add additional folders to the one currently being viewed.

Hot tip

Click or tap on the **Options** button on the View Menu to set additional options for the operation of a folder and how items are displayed within it.

75

Library menu options

If there is a down-pointing arrow next to an item on a Library menu click or tap on it to see additional options, such as the **Optimize library for** button, which optimizes the folder for specific types of content.

Switching Users

If you have a number of user accounts defined on the computer (several accounts can be active at the same time) you do not need to close your apps and log off to be able to switch to another user and it is easy to switch back and forth. To do this:

Don't forget

All of your settings and files are maintained but the new user will not be able to see them; and you will not be able to see theirs when you switch back. Your screen will look exactly the same as you left it.

1 Click or tap on the name of the current active user in the top right-hand corner of the Start screen

2 Click on another user's name. They will have to enter their own password in order to access their account, at which point they will be signed in. You can then switch between users without each having to log out each time

As an alternative way to switch users:

1 Press **WinKey + L** to lock the current user

2 Access the login screen for all of the current users and select one as required

Shut Down

When you turn off your computer (see Chapter Two), you will be warned if there are other user accounts still logged on to the computer.

Beware

If the other accounts have data files open, shutting down without logging them off could cause them to lose information.

1 Click or tap on the **Shut down anyway** button to shut down without other users logging off

Someone else is still using this PC. If you shut down now, they could lose unsaved work.

Shut down anyway

4 Working with Apps

In Windows 8, some apps are pre-installed, while hundreds more can be downloaded from the Windows Store. This chapter shows how to work with and organize apps in Windows 8 and how to find your way around the Windows Store and obtain apps.

Starting with Apps

The word 'app' may be seen by some as a new-fangled piece of techno-speak. But, simply, it means a computer program. Originally, apps were items that were downloaded to smartphones and tablet computers. However, the terminology has now been expanded to cover any computer program. So, in Windows 8 most programs are referred to as apps, although some legacy ones may still be referred to as programs.

There are three clear types of apps within Windows 8:

- **New Windows 8 apps.** These are the built-in apps that appear on the Start screen. They cover the areas of communication, entertainment and information and several of them are linked together through the online sharing service SkyDrive

- **Windows apps.** These are the old-style Windows apps that people may be familiar with from previous versions of Windows. These open in the Desktop environment

- **Windows Store apps.** These are apps that can be downloaded from the online Windows Store and cover a wide range of subjects and functionality. Some Windows Store apps are free while others have to be paid for

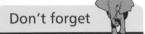

Don't forget

The new Windows 8 apps open with the Windows 8 interface, rather than the more traditional Windows interface used with previous versions of Windows. However, the older Windows apps still use the previous interface.

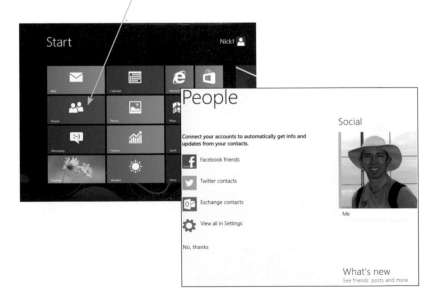

New Windows 8 apps

Windows 8 apps are accessed from the brightly-colored tiles on the Start screen. Click or tap on a tile to open the relevant app:

Windows apps

The Windows apps are generally the ones that appeared as default with previous versions of Windows and would have been accessed from the Start Button. The Windows apps can be accessed from the Start screen by right-clicking on the screen and clicking on the **All apps** button on the bottom toolbar (see page 83 for more information about this). When Windows apps are opened from the Start screen they have the traditional Windows look and functionality. Windows apps open on the Desktop.

Don't forget

The **All apps** button can be accessed on a touch screen laptop by swiping up from the bottom of the Start screen. It can also be accessed by pressing **WinKey + Z** on a keyboard.

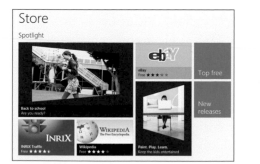

Windows Store apps

The Windows Store apps are accessed and downloaded from the online Windows Store. Apps can be browsed and searched for in the Store and when they are downloaded they are added to the Start screen.

Don't forget

The Windows Store is accessed by clicking or tapping on the **Store** tile on the Start screen.

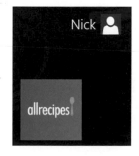

Windows 8 Apps

The new Windows 8 apps that are accessed directly from the Start screen cover a range of communication, entertainment and information functions. The apps are:

 Calendar. This can be used to add appointments and important dates. It is closely integrated with the Mail, Messaging and People apps.

 Camera. This can be used to take photos directly onto your desktop, laptop or tablet computer, but only if it has a built-in camera attached.

 Desktop. This takes you to the Desktop facility that has been available in previous versions of Windows.

 Finance. This is one of the information apps that provides real-time financial news.

 Games. This can be used to play online Xbox games, either individually or by connecting to other online user.

 Internet Explorer. This is the Windows 8 version of the widely-used web browser. This version is IE 10 and the Windows 8 version has a different interface from the Desktop one.

 Mail. This is the online Mail facility. You can use it to connect to a selection of online Mail accounts, e.g. Outlook (previously Hotmail) and GMail.

 Maps. This provides online access to maps from around the world. It enables locations to be viewed in Road or Aerial view and can also show traffic conditions for specific areas.

 Messaging. This is the online messaging service that can be used to send free text messages to other users with a compatible service. Messages can also include photos and videos.

Don't forget

See Chapter Five for more information about working with Internet Explorer 10 in Windows 8 and Desktop mode.

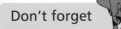

Don't forget

See Chapter Six for details about working with the Calendar, Messaging and People apps.

Music. This can be used to access the online Music Store where music can be previewed and downloaded. It can be also used to organize and play the music on your computer.

 News. This is one of the information apps that provides real-time news information. This is based on your location as entered at installation.

 People. This is the address book app for adding contacts. Your contacts from sites such as Facebook and Twitter can also be imported.

 Photos. This can be used to view and organize your photos. You can also share and print photos directly from the Photos app.

 SkyDrive. This is an online facility for storing and sharing content from your computer. This includes photos, documents and settings.

 Sport. This is one of the information apps that provides real-time sports news.

 Store. This provides access to the online Windows Store from where a range of other apps can be bought and downloaded to your computer.

Travel. This is one of the information apps that provides travel news and features.

 Video. This can be used to access the online Video Store where videos can be previewed and downloaded.

Weather. This provides real-time weather forecasts for locations around the world. By default it will provide the nearest forecast to your location as entered when you installed Windows 8.

Don't forget

The information for the Finance, News, Sports and Travel apps is provided by Bing.

Don't forget

SkyDrive can also be used to share your content, such as photos and documents, with other people. See Chapter Six for details.

Using Windows 8 Apps

The appearance of the new Windows 8 apps is different from those that have been provided with previous versions of Windows. Their functionality is slightly different too in that the toolbars and settings are hidden and only appear when required.

Accessing toolbars

To access toolbars in Windows 8 apps:

Don't forget

The bottom toolbar can be accessed on a touch screen laptop by swiping up from the bottom, or down from the top, of the screen in the relevant app. It can also be accessed pressing **WinKey + Z** on a keyboard.

1   Right-click anywhere on the **app**

2   The toolbar appears at the bottom of the screen. This is relevant to the individual app. Therefore, the toolbar will be different for the Photos and the Mail apps and so on

Accessing settings

Settings for individual Windows 8 apps can be accessed from the Settings Charm (the relevant app has to be the current one being used to view its settings):

Beware

Check at the top of the Settings panel to ensure that you have accessed the settings for the correct app.

1   Move the cursor over the bottom or top right-hand corner and click or tap on the **Settings Charm**

2   The Settings options for the current app are displayed. Click or tap on each option to see the available settings for that item

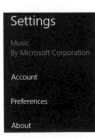

Settings

Music
By Microsoft Corporation

Account

Preferences

About

Viewing All Apps

There is a lot more to Windows 8 than the default Windows 8 apps. Most of the system Windows apps that were available with previous versions of Windows are still here, just not initially visible on the Start screen. However, it only takes two clicks on the Start screen to view all of the apps on your computer.

Don't forget

On a touch screen laptop, swipe up from the bottom, or down from the top, of the screen to view the **All apps** button.

1 Right-click anywhere on the **Start** screen

2 Click or tap on the **All apps** button in the bottom right-hand corner

Don't forget

Apps that are installed from a CD or DVD are automatically included on the Start screen, not just from the All apps screen.

3 All of the apps are displayed. Scroll to the right to view all of the available apps

Beware

When you move away from the All apps screen the apps disappear from the Start screen. You have to access the **All apps** button each time you return to the Start screen and want to view the full range of available apps.

4 Click or tap on an app to open it

Closing Windows 8 Apps

Because they have a different interface from traditional Windows apps, it is not always immediately obvious how to close a Windows 8 app. There are three ways in which this can be done:

Closing with the App Switcher sidebar

To close a Windows 8 app from the App Switcher sidebar:

1 Move the cursor over the top left-hand corner of the screen and drag down to view all of the currently-open Windows 8 apps

2 Right-click on the app you want to close and click or tap on the **Close** button

Closing by dragging

To close a Windows 8 app by dragging it off the screen:

1 Move the cursor to the top of the screen until the pointer changes into a hand

2 Click, or tap, and hold at the top of the screen with the hand and drag down to the bottom of the screen

3 Release the mouse at the bottom of the screen and the app will disappear

Closing with the keyboard

To close a Windows 8 app by just using the keyboard:

1 With the current app active, press **Alt + F4**

Searching for Apps

As you acquire more and more apps, it may become harder to always find the ones you want. To help with this you can use the Search Charm to search over all of the apps on your computer. To do this:

 Move the cursor over the top or bottom right-hand corner of the screen and select the **Search Charm**

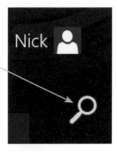

Enter a word in the Search box and select **Apps** from the list below the Search box

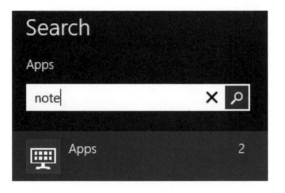

As you type, relevant apps are displayed. When the one you are seeking appears, click or tap on it to start the app

Hot tip

You only have to put in the first couple of letters of an app and Search will automatically suggest results based on this. The more that you type, the more specific the results become. Case does not matter when you are entering a search word.

Pin to Start Screen

In most cases you will want to have quick access to a variety of apps on the Start screen, not just the new Windows 8 apps. It is possible to pin any app to the Start screen so that it is always readily available. To do this:

1 Access **All apps** as shown on page 83

2 Right-click on an app to select it, so that there is a tick showing in the top right-hand corner

3 When the app is selected, the bottom toolbar appears. Click or tap on the **Pin to Start** button

4 The app is pinned to the Start screen. It can now be repositioned, if required, as with any other app, as shown in Chapter Three

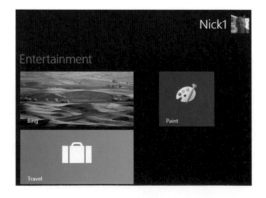

Hot tip

When an app is selected, right-click on it again to de-select it. The bottom toolbar also disappears when this is done.

Hot tip

Apps can be unpinned from the Start screen by right-clicking on them and selecting **Unpin from Start** from the bottom toolbar. This applies to all apps.

Pin to Taskbar

Since most of the Windows system apps open on the Desktop you may want to have quick access to them here. This can be done by pinning them to the Desktop Taskbar (the bar that appears along the bottom of the Desktop). To do this:

1 Access **All apps** as shown on page 83

2 Right-click on an app to select it, so that there is a tick showing in the top right-hand corner

3 When the app is selected, the bottom toolbar appears. Click or tap on the **Pin to taskbar** button

4 Open apps on the Taskbar can also be pinned here by right-clicking on them and selecting **Pin this app to the taskbar**

5 Pinned items remain on the Taskbar even once they have been closed

Hot tip

Apps can be unpinned from the Taskbar by right-clicking on them and selecting **Unpin this program from taskbar** from the contextual menu.

Apps on the Desktop

The Windows system apps open on the Desktop, in the same way as with previous versions of Windows, even though they are opened from the Start screen.

Opening a Windows system app

To open a Windows system app:

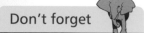

Don't forget

Windows system apps here refers to any apps that are not part of the Windows 8 interface. Within this group there are some apps known specifically as Windows System apps.

1 Right-click on the Start screen and click or tap on the **All apps** button

2 Select the app you want to open

3 The app opens on the Desktop

Hot tip

If apps have been pinned to the Taskbar, as shown on page 87, they can be opened directly from here by clicking or tapping on them.

4 Click or tap on the tabs at the top of the app to access relevant toolbars and menus

Closing a Windows system app
There are several ways to close a Windows system app:

 Click or tap on the red **Close** button in the top right of the window

 Select **File>Exit** from the File menu

89

Press **Alt+F4**

Right-click on the icon on the Taskbar and select **Close window**

Recent
- Windows8

- WordPad
- Pin this program to taskbar
- Close window

If any changes have been made to the document, you may receive a warning message advising you to Save the associated file

WordPad ✕
Do you want to save changes to Document?

Save   Don't Save   Cancel

Using the Windows Store

The third category of apps that can be used with Windows 8 are those that are downloaded from the online Windows Store. These cover a wide range of topics and it is an excellent way to add functionality to Windows 8. To use the Windows Store:

Don't forget

The Windows 8 apps can all be downloaded directly from the Windows Store.

Don't forget

Apps can be searched for in the Windows Store in the same way you search for them on your laptop as shown on page 85. Instead of selecting the Apps button to search over, select the Store button.

1 Click or tap on the **Store** tile on the Start screen

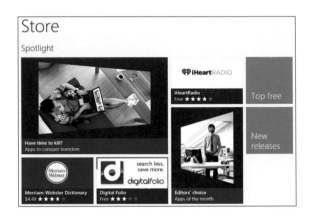

2 The currently-featured apps are displayed on the home screen

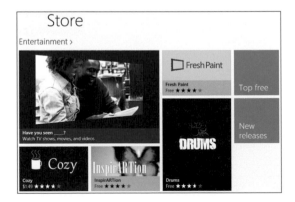

3 Scroll to the right to see additional categories of apps

4 Click or tap on one of the green boxes to see the apps for that specific heading, e.g. Top free apps

5 The icons for the apps are displayed

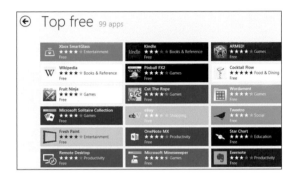

6 Click or tap on a category and select an app to preview

Don't forget

On the preview screen, click on the **Details** link to view details about the computer requirements for the app and the **Reviews** link to see what other people think.

7 Scroll here to preview additional pages about the app

...cont'd

8 Move the cursor over the bottom right-hand corner of the screen and click or tap here to minimize the app categories

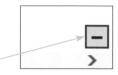

9 Click or tap on a category to access it (it automatically enlarges on the screen from its minimized state)

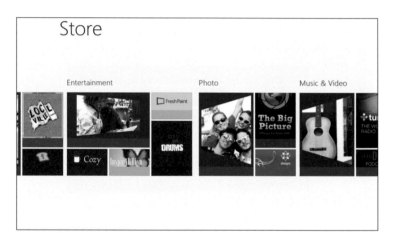

Hot tip

To return to the Home screen at any point, right-click anywhere on the Store screen and click or tap on the green **Home** button from the top toolbar.

Home

10 Each category has options such as Top Free. If there are new releases for the category, these will be shown under the Top free button

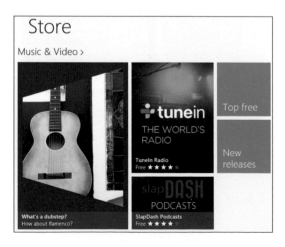

Buying Apps

When you find an app that you want to use you can download it to your computer or tablet. To do this:

1 Access the **Overview** screen for the app and click or tap on the **Install** button

2 To download apps from the Windows Store you need to have a Microsoft Account. Enter your details and click or tap on the **Sign in** button

3 The app is added to the Start screen and placed in the next space in the group to the furthest right on the Start screen

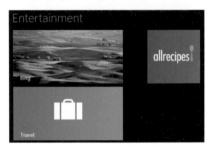

4 Click or tap on the app to open it and use it

Don't forget

If there is a fee for an app, this will be displayed on, or next to, the **Install** button.

Don't forget

Once apps have been downloaded they can be reorganized and moved into different groups on the Start screen, or dragged away from their default group to start a new one.

Don't forget

To view the apps that you have downloaded, right-click on the Windows Store Home screen and click or tap on the Your apps link at the top of the page.

Install and Uninstall

Installing apps from a CD or DVD

If the app you want to install is provided on a CD or DVD, you normally just insert the disc. The installation app starts up automatically and you can follow the instructions to select features and complete the installation.

If the installation does not start automatically, you can Run it from File Explorer by accessing the Setup.exe file. This should start the installation process. To do this:

1 Right-click on the Start screen and click or tap on the **All apps** button

2 Select the **File Explorer** app

3 Access the CD or DVD in File Explorer

4 Access the **Setup.exe** file and double-click or tap on it to run it. Follow the on-screen prompts to install the app

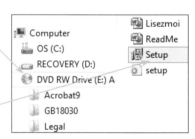

5 Apps that are installed from a CD or DVD are automatically pinned to the Start screen

...cont'd

Uninstalling apps

In previous versions of Windows, apps were uninstalled through the Control Panel. However, in Windows 8 they can be uninstalled directly from the Start screen. To do this:

1. Right-click on an app to select it, as denoted by the tick in the top right-hand corner

2. Click or tap on the **Uninstall** button on the toolbar at the bottom of the screen

3. A window alerts you to the fact that related information will be removed if the app is uninstalled. Click or tap on the **Uninstall** button to continue

This app and its related info will be removed from this PC.

Allrecipes

Uninstall

4. If the app is a new Windows 8 one, or has been pinned to the Start screen, its tile will be removed from the Start screen. For other apps, they will no longer be available from the All apps option

Don't forget

If apps have been installed from a CD or DVD they can also still be uninstalled from within the Control Panel. To do this, select the **Programs** options and click or tap on the **Uninstall a Program** link. The installed apps will be displayed. Select one of the apps and click or tap on the **Uninstall/Change** link to remove it.

Don't forget

Some elements of Windows 8, such as the Control Panel, still refer to apps as programs, but they are the same thing.

95

Using Live Tiles

Before any of the Windows 8 apps have been used, they are depicted on the Start screen with tiles of solid color. However, once you open an app it activates the Live Tile feature (if it is supported by that app). This enables the tile to display real-time information from the app, even when it is not the app currently being used. This means that you can view information from your apps directly from the Start screen. To use Live Tiles:

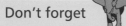
1 Right-click on a tile to select it. If it has Live Tile functionality, click or tap on the **Turn live tile on** button to activate this

2 Live Tiles display real-time text and images from the selected apps. These are updated when there is new information available via the app

3 To turn off a Live Tile, right-click on a tile to select it and click or tap on the **Turn live tile off** button

5 Internet and Email

Internet Explorer, the widely-used Microsoft web browser, has been redesigned for Windows 8. The latest version, IE 10, can be used with different interfaces whether in Windows 8 mode or the Desktop mode. This chapter looks at the difference between the two and also shows how to use your laptop for online tasks such as booking a vacation and also working with email.

Connecting to the Internet

The Internet is now a ubiquitous part of our lives. We use it for everything from viewing the news, to shopping, to online genealogy. With a laptop the possibilities for accessing the Internet are expanded to almost any location, not just when you are at home. However, for all users it is first necessary to set up a home Internet connection. To do this you will need:

- An Internet Service Provider (ISP), to provide an account that gives you access to the Internet

- A transmission network – cable, telephone or wireless

- Some hardware to link into that transmission network

- For a broadband connection, such as Digital Subscriber Line (DSL) or cable, you need a DSL or Cable modem or router, usually provided by the ISP

- For dial-up connection, you need a dial-up modem, which is usually pre-installed on your laptop

In many cases, Windows 8 will recognize the elements required to connect to the Internet and do this automatically. However, you can also do this through the Control Panel:

Don't forget

For a comprehensive guide to using the Internet, see "Internet for Seniors in easy steps" in this series.

Don't forget

There are hundreds of ISPs. Type "ISP" into Google to find an extensive list.

1 Access the **Control Panel** and select the **View network Status and tasks** link, under the Network and Internet heading. This opens in the Network and Sharing Center

2 Click or tap on the **Setup a new connection or network** link to display the connection options supported

3 Select **Connect to the Internet** and click or tap the **Next** button

Set Up a Connection or Network

Choose a connection option

Connect to the Internet
Set up a broadband or dial-up connection to the Internet

Set up a new network
Set up a new router or access point.

Manually connect to a wireless network
Connect to a hidden network or create a new wireless profile.

Connect to a workplace
Set up a dial-up or VPN connection to your workplace.

Next   Cancel

4 The Connect to the Internet wizard launches. Select the appropriate connection method

Connect to the Internet

How do you want to connect?

Broadband (PPPoE)
Connect using DSL or cable that requires a user name and password.

Dial-up
Connect using a dial-up modem or ISDN.

Cancel

Windows identifies all of the possible connection methods based on the hardware configuration of your laptop. If you have a wireless router or network, you may have an option for Wireless connection. If there is no dial-up modem installed, then the Dial-up connection method will not be available.

Don't forget

Continue through the wizard to complete the definition of your Internet connection, ready to start browsing the Internet.

IE 10 in Windows 8 Mode

The default web browser, for connecting to the World Wide Web (WWW), provided with Windows 8 is Internet Explorer (IE) 10. However, there is a slight twist as it is a two-for-one browser in many respects: there is one version for the new Windows 8 interface and another Desktop version which will be more familiar to anyone who has used previous versions of IE.

IE 10 for Windows 8 mode is optimized to display the maximum amount of screen estate, without a lot of clutter in terms of toolbars. It is also designed for touch screen use, although you can use it perfectly well with a mouse and keyboard too.

1 To open the new Windows 8 version of IE 10, click or tap on this tile on the Start screen

2 The IE 10 toolbars are hidden so that the web pages can be viewed with the whole screen

3 Right-click on the screen, or swipe down from the top or up from the bottom of the screen, to access the Tab Switcher at the top of the screen and the Navigation Bar at the bottom.
Click or tap once on the screen or swipe upwards on the Tab Switcher to hide these items

Opening Pages

The Navigation Bar that can be accessed at the bottom of the screen (see previous page) can be used to open new web pages.

1 Type a web address in the Address Bar. When you click or tap in the Address Bar, icons of the pages that you have visited are available. Click or tap on one to open it

2 As you start typing a web address in the Address Bar, suggestions appear above it. These change as you add more letters in the Address Bar. Click or tap on one of the suggestions if you want to open that page

Hot tip

If you are entering a web address into IE 10 you do not require the initial "www:". As you start typing the address, suggestions will appear.

Navigating Pages

Because of the simplified interface for IE 10 in Windows 8 mode there is not the range of functionality of the Desktop version. However, this also means that pages can be navigated efficiently with a few clicks or taps.

1 Use these buttons on the Navigation Bar at the bottom of the screen to, from left to right, Refresh/Stop the current page, pin the page to the Start screen and to access page tools

2 When moving between different web pages, move the cursor over the left edge and click or tap on the **Back** arrow. Do the same at the opposite side of the screen for the **Forward** button

3 Click or tap on this button on the Address Bar for the Back function (the **Forward** button is on the other side)

Pinning a Web Page

If you have favorite web pages that you visit often it can be frustrating having to access them through IE 10 each time. A solution to this is to pin a link to the Start screen. This means that you can access the page directly from the Start screen; IE 10 will be opened at the selected page. To pin a web page:

 Open the required web page and click or tap on this button on the Address Bar

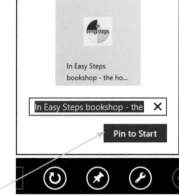

 **Don't forget**

Access the IE 10 Address Bar by right-clicking on a web page or swiping up from the bottom, or down from the top, of the screen.

2 Click or tap on the **Pin to Start** button. (Enter the accompanying text if required. This will appear on the Start screen tile)

3 The link to the page is added to the Start screen as a new tile. Click or tap on this to open the page directly from the Start screen

Tabs in Windows 8 Mode

Tabs within web browsers are now an established part of our online experience. This enables multiple web pages to be open in the same window. Each tab can have its own content displayed. In IE 10 in Windows 8 mode, tabs are accommodated by the Tab Switcher that is accessed at the top of the screen by right-clicking on the main screen, or dragging down from the top of the screen on a touch screen device. To work with tabs in IE 10 in Windows 8 mode:

1. Click or tap on this button at the top right-hand corner of the Tab Switcher to add a new tab

2. Open a web page in the regular way

3. The open tabs are displayed on the Tab Switcher. Click or tap on a tab to access that page. Click or tap on the cross on the tab thumbnail to close a tab

Beware

InPrivate browsing leaves no record of the browser session, in terms of pages visited. Therefore it is not a good option if children are using it.

4. Click or tap on this button to open an InPrivate Browsing tab or close all of the currently-open tabs

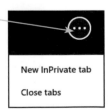
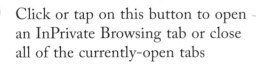

IE 10 Windows 8 Settings

As with other Windows 8 apps, IE 10 in Windows 8 mode has its own settings which are accessed from the Settings Charm.

1 Open a web page in IE 10 for Windows 8. Move the cursor over the bottom right-hand corner (or swipe from the side of the screen) and click or tap on the **Settings Charm**

2 Click or tap on the **Internet Options** link

3 Options can be applied for deleting the browsing history, whether websites have to ask permission if they are trying to use your physical location, the zoom settings for sites, turning on the Flip ahead functionality and encoding options if a page is not displaying correctly

IE 10 on the Desktop

IE 10 for the Desktop will have a more familiar look and feel to users of previous versions of IE and it also has a wider range of functionality. The main ways to access it are:

1 Access the Internet Explorer icon on the Taskbar

2 Within IE 10 in Windows 8 mode, click or tap on the **Page Tools** button and click or tap on the **View on the desktop** link

The Desktop version of IE 10 includes:

Menu bar   Address bar (with URL)   Favorites bar   Tabbed browsing (multipage)

Page content

Menu bar

At the top of the browser window is the Menu bar that contains sections with much of the functionality of IE 10. Click or tap on one of the headings to view the additional options. If there is an arrow next to an item it means that there are more options for this item.

Browser controls
The Desktop version of IE 10 has considerable functionality:

Back and Forward
Select the **back** and **forward** buttons
to switch between recently-visited web
pages, or hold on one of the buttons to
view the Recent Pages list.

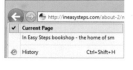

Tabs
Tabs allow you to view multiple web pages
in the same Internet Explorer window.

The Address Bar
This is where web addresses
are entered and includes

access to the Search box, a page compatibility view and the
Refresh and **Stop** buttons to control the loading of the
web page specified in the address box. This changes to the
Go To button when a web address is entered.

The Search Box
The Address Bar can also be used as a
Search Box. To do this, enter a word
in the Address Bar. In the results
window, click or tap on the **Turn On
Suggestions**. The results will be
displayed as links to web pages and search suggestions.

Command Bar
This is accessed from the
View>Toolbars option
on the Menu bar and has items for setting the Home page,
RSS feeds, reading emails, printing, page information and
safety items such as InPrivate Browsing, and web page tools.

Favorites Button and Favorites Center
The Favorites button displays the Favorites
Center, with the favorites, feeds and
website history.

107

Don't forget

InPrivate Browsing is
a way of viewing web
pages without any of
the information being
stored by the browser.
For instance, it will
not show up in your
browsing history or
store cookies.

Bookmark Favorites

If you see a web page that you want to revisit, add it to your Favorites list to save having to record or remember the address.

1 While viewing the page, click or tap on the **Favorites** button (see page 107) and then click or tap on the **Add to Favorites** button (or press **Ctrl+D**)

Add to favorites ▼	✕
Add to favorites...	Ctrl+D

2 The page title is used as the name for the new favorite, but you can type an alternative name if you wish

Add a Favorite
Add this webpage as a favorite. To access your favorites, visit the Favorites Center.
Name: PC Gaming - Microsoft Store Online
Create in: ⭐ Favorites ▾ New folder
Add Cancel

3 Select **Add** to save the details in your Favorites list

View Favorites

1 Select the Favorites Center button and click or tap on the **Favorites** button (if not already selected)

Add to favorites ▼
Favorites | Feeds | History
📁 Favorites Bar
PC Gaming - Microsoft Store Online

2 Click or tap on a folder name to expand it

3 Click or tap any Favorites entry to display that page

4 Click or tap on **Add to favorites** and **Organize favorites** to move, rename or delete the entries

Add to favorites ▼	✕
Add to favorites...	Ctrl+D
Add to Favorites bar	
Add current tabs to favorites...	
Import and export...	
Organize favorites...	

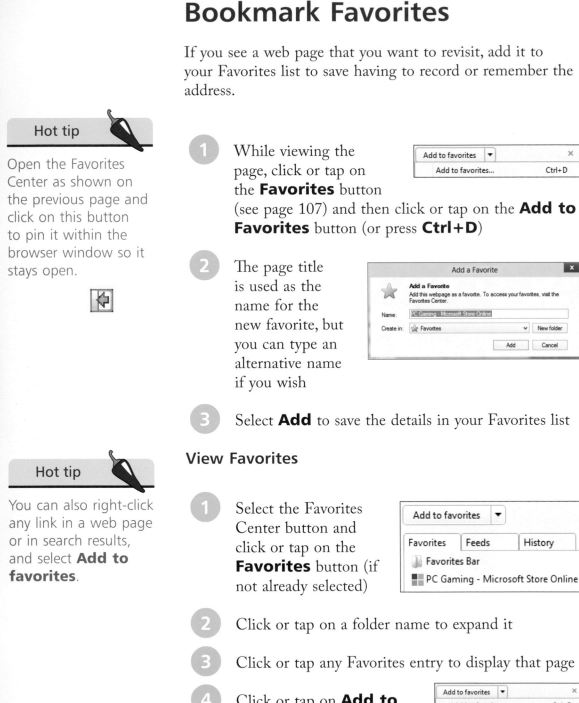

Home Page

Your home page is displayed when you start Internet Explorer or when you click the Home button. The web page displayed may be the Windows default, or may have been defined by your ISP or your computer supplier. However, you can choose any web page as your home page.

Current Web Page

1. With the preferred web page displayed, select the arrow next to the **Home** button on the Command bar and select **Add or change home page**

2. Select **Use this webpage as your only home page** or select another option

Reset Home Page

1. Select **Tools>Internet Options** and select the **General** tab

2. Select **Use default** to use the default home page specified by Internet Explorer

   or

   Select **Use new tab** to specify a home page for when a new tab is created

3. Click or tap **OK** to save the changes

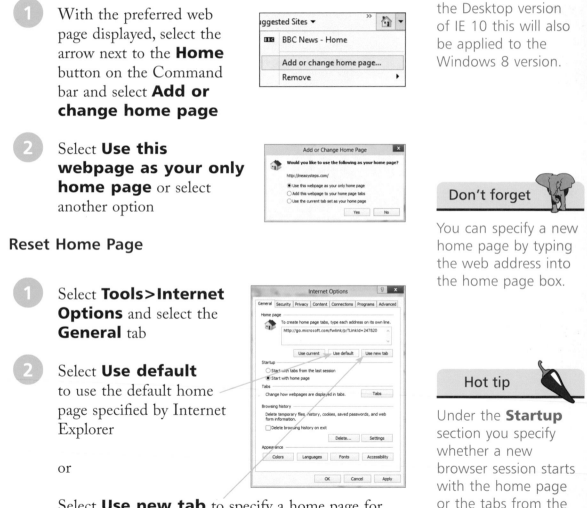

Hot tip

If a page is set as your only home page in the Desktop version of IE 10 this will also be applied to the Windows 8 version.

Don't forget

You can specify a new home page by typing the web address into the home page box.

Hot tip

Under the **Startup** section you specify whether a new browser session starts with the home page or the tabs from the last session.

Tabbed Browsing

You can open multiple websites in a single browser window, with each web page on a separate tab.

Don't forget

To open a web page link in a new tab, press **Ctrl** as you click or right-click the link (or press and hold on the link) and select **Open in new tab**.

1 To open another tab, click or tap on the **New Tab** button

2 Type an address in the Address Bar and press **Enter** or click or tap on one of the frequently visited sites

Hot tip

Right-click on a tab at the top of the browser window for a menu of options relating to the tab, even if it is not currently active.

3 To switch between tabs, select the page tab on the tab row

4 Close IE 10 and you will be asked if you want to **Close all tabs** or just **Close current tab**

Hot tip

To save the group of tabs for reuse at any time, click or tap on **Add to favorites** (see page 108) and select **Add current tabs to favorites**.

5 You can Reopen closed tabs from a new tab, by clicking or tapping on the **Reopen closed tabs** link and selecting the tab, or tabs, that you want to reopen

Downloading New Browsers

There are several other browsers that can be used to view the Web. These include Mozilla Firefox, Google Chrome and Opera. It is possible to download the Firefox browser for free to view the Web. To do this:

1 Go to the Firefox download page at www.mozilla.org

2 Click or tap on this button to begin the downloading process

3 Click or tap on the **Run** button and complete the installation screens

4 Once the installation is complete the Firefox browser can be opened by clicking on this icon

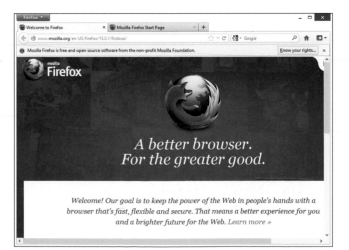

Don't forget

Chrome can be downloaded at www.google.com/chrome

111

Beware

All new browsers should be free to download. If you are asked for a fee, cancel the process and look for another browser.

Shopping on Your Laptop

Some people love physically going around shops, while for others it is a chore. For the latter group, online shopping is one of the great innovations of the Web, and even for the former group it can be invaluable when there is not the time or opportunity to go to physical shops. With a laptop, it is possible to do your shopping in the comfort of your own home while avoiding the crowds.

When you are shopping online there are some guidelines that you should follow to try and ensure you are in a safe online environment and do not spend too much money:

- Make a note of what you want to buy and stick to this once you have found it. Online shopping sites are adept at displaying a lot of enticing offers and it is a lot easier to buy something by clicking a button than it is to physically take it to a checkout

- Never buy anything that is promoted to you via an email, unless it is from a company whom you have asked to send you promotional information

- When paying for items, make sure that the online site has a secure area for accepting payment and credit-card details. A lot of sites display information about this within their payment area, and another way to ascertain this to check in the address bar of the payment page. If it is within a secure area the address of the page will start with "https" rather than the standard "http"

Don't forget

A lot of online shopping sites list recommendations for you based on what you have already looked at or bought on the site. This is done by using "cookies", which are small programs that are downloaded from the site and then track the items that you look at on the site.

Using online shopping

The majority of online shopping sites are similar in their operation:

- Goods are identified

- Goods are placed in a shopping basket

- Once the shopping is completed you proceed to the checkout

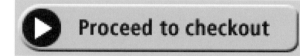

- You enter your shipping details and pay for the goods, usually with a credit card

On some sites you have to register before you can buy goods and in some cases this enables you to perform your shopping more quickly by using a one-click system. This means that all of your billing and payment details are already stored on the site and you can buy goods simply by clicking one button without having to re-enter your details. One of the most prominent sites to use this method is Amazon:

Beware

One-click shopping is an effective way to spend money very quickly. However, you usually have a period of time in which you can cancel your purchases after you have bought them in this way.

113

Booking a Vacation

Just as a lot of retailers have created an online presence, the same is also true for vacation companies and travel agents. It is now possible to book almost any type of vacation on the Web, from cruises to city breaks.

Several sites offer full travel services where they can deal with flights, hotels, insurance, car hire and excursions. These sites include:

- www.expedia.com
- www.travelocity.com
- www.tripadvisor.com

These sites usually list special offers and last-minute deals on their home pages and there is also a facility for specifying your precise requirements. To do this:

Hot tip

It is always worth searching different sites to get the best possible prices. In some cases, it is cheapest to buy different elements of a vacation from different sites, e.g. flights from one and accommodation from another.

114

1 Select your vacation requirements

2 Enter flight details (if applicable)

3 Enter dates for your vacation

4 Click on the **Search** button

SEARCH FOR FLIGHT + HOTEL

- ● Flight + Hotel
- ○ Flight + Hotel + Car
- ○ Flight + Car
- ○ Hotel + Car

Search two destinations »

Leaving from:	Departing:
New York, NY, United States (NYC -	11/13/2012

Going to:	Returning:
Honolulu, Hawaii, United States of A	11/27/2012

☐ I only need a hotel for part of my trip

Rooms:
1 ∨

Room 1:

Adults (18-64)	Seniors (65+)	Children (0-17)
2 ∨	0 ∨	0 ∨

In addition to sites that do everything for you it is also possible to book your vacation on individual sites. This can be particularly useful for cruises and also for booking hotels around the world. Some websites to look at are:

Cruises

- www.cruises.com
- www.carnival.com
- www.princess.com

Don't forget

Vacation and hotel websites usually have versions that are specific to your geographical location.

Hotels

- www.hotels.com
- www.booking.com
- www.choicehotels.com

Researching Family History

A recent growth industry on the web has been family history, or genealogy. Hundreds of organizations around the world have now digitized their records concerning individuals and family histories and there are numerous websites that provide online access to these records. Some of these sites are:

- www.ancestry.com

- www.genealogy.com

- www.familysearch.org

- www.rootsweb.ancestry.com

116

Most genealogy sites require you to register, for a fee, before you can conduct extensive family research on their sites, but once you do the process is similar on them all.

1 Enter the details of the family members in the search boxes

Ready to make your first discovery?

It's not just history. It's your history. So start with yourself and we'll help you find more about your heritage.

Your name* | Vandome | Nick | **Age*** 47

Your father

Gender ⦿ Male ◯ Female

Email

Choose who to search for:
⦿ Father's family ◯ Mother's family ◯ Someone else

Your mother

Get started 🔒 We value your privacy. Read our privacy policy

2 Click on the **Get started** button

Get started

3 The results are displayed for the names searched against

Father's information

Your father's name
Peter | Vandome

His birth year 1934 ☑ A guess   **His birthplace** London, London, England   ☑ Still living

Your father's siblings
First names separated by commas

Your father's father First | Last   **Your father's mother** First | Maiden name

Bonus: improve your search with more information
My grandfather's ⇕ | choose... ⇕ | was...

Search for Records

Don't forget

Some sites offer a free initial search, but after that you will have to pay for each search.

4 Click on the **Search for Records** button to get a detailed report for your information. This may require registering on the site

Search for Records

5 On some sites there is a facility for creating your family tree. Enter the relevant details

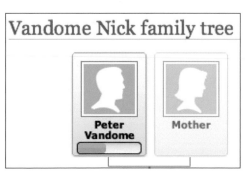

Vandome Nick family tree

Peter Vandome

Mother

Setting Up Mail

Email has become an essential part of everyday life, both socially and in the business world. Windows 8 accommodates this with the Mail app. This can be used to link to online services such as GMail and Outlook (the renamed version of Hotmail) and also other email accounts. To set up an email account with Mail:

1 Click or tap on the **Mail** tile on the Start screen

2 Access the **Settings Charm**

3 Click or tap on the **Accounts** link

4 Click or tap on the **Add an account** button

5 Select the type of account to which you want to link via the Mail app. This can be an online email account that you have already set up

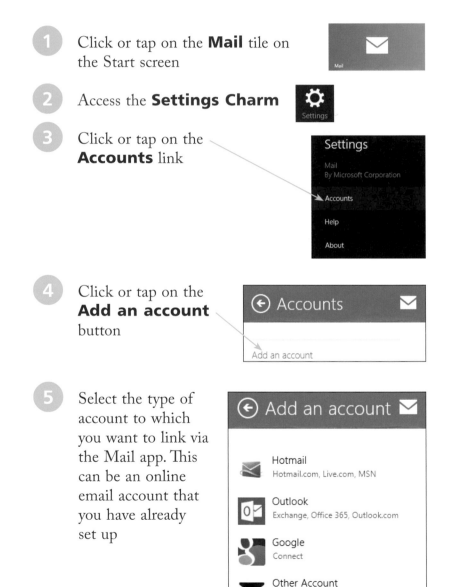

Settings

Mail
By Microsoft Corporation

Accounts

Help

About

⟵ Accounts ✉

Add an account

⟵ Add an account ✉

Hotmail
Hotmail.com, Live.com, MSN

Outlook
Exchange, Office 365, Outlook.com

Google
Connect

Other Account
Connect

6 Enter your current login details for the selected email account and click or tap on the **Connect** button

Add your Google account

Enter the information below to connect to your Google account.

Email address

nickvandome@googlemail.com

Password

••••••••

Connect   Cancel

7 Once it has been connected, the details of the account are shown under the Mail heading, including the mailboxes within the account. Click or tap on the Inbox to view the emails within it

Mail

Google   11

Inbox 11

Drafts

Sent items

Outbox

Junk

Deleted items

8 The list of emails appears in the left-hand pane. Click or tap on a message to view it in the reading pane. Click or tap on this button to go back to the main Inbox window

Google Inbox

Today's Top 5 Investing Ideas
One of the Best Ways to Bui... Thu

Today's Top 5 Investing Ideas
One of the Best Ways to Build a Dividend Portfolio I've Ever Seen
To: Nick Vandome

Facebook
You have more friends on F... Wed

Today's Top 5 Investing I...
The Best Income Stocks Y... Wed

STREETAUTHORITY

TODAY'S TOP 5 INVESTING IDEAS

Today's Top 5 Investing Id...
How to get Yields of 13.8... Tue

Fill Up Your Car For $2.14 a Gallon
There is a trend popping up on the nation's highways of fueling stations offering transportation fuel at a 43% discount. And investors in the company making it possible stand to make a killing...

Today's Top 5 Investing I...
The Housing Recovery is... Mon

Today's Top 5 Investing Id...
Billionaires Dump Stocks (... Sun

Is it Time for You to Finally Sell Coca-Cola?
Short sellers are flocking to this stock, which doesn't make sense, until you dig a little deeper.

Today's Top 5 Investing Ideas
This Famous Investor Spent... Sat

One of the Best Ways to Build a Dividend Portfolio I've Ever Seen
This high-yielding investment is a great low-risk opportunity that rewards its investors with generous dividends.

Today's Top 5 Investing I...
This Famous Investor Sp... 8/22/12

Facebook
You have more friends... 8/21/12

The Surprising Place where the Wealthiest 6% Make Their Millions [sponsor]
Most people don't even realize this exists... but there's a private stock market where politicians, rock stars, and royalty have made their fortunes for years. And now, you can too. We'll show you how, here.

Today's Top 5 Investin...
The 'Sweet Spot' of Inv... 8/21/12

Today's Top 5 Investin...
Here's What the Top F... 8/20/12

Working with Mail

Once you have set up an account in the Mail app you then start creating and managing your emails with it.

1 On the Inbox page, select an email and click or tap on this button to respond

2 Select an email and click or tap on this button to delete it

Composing email
To compose and send an email message:

1 Click or tap on this button to create a new message

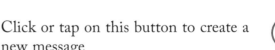

2 Click or tap in the To field and enter an email address

Don't forget

Contacts that are added automatically as email recipients are taken from the People app, providing there is an email address connected to their entry here.

---

3 Click or tap on the **More details** link to access options for blind copying and priority level

4 The email address can be in the format of myname@gmail.com or enter the name of one of your contacts in the People app and the email address will be entered automatically

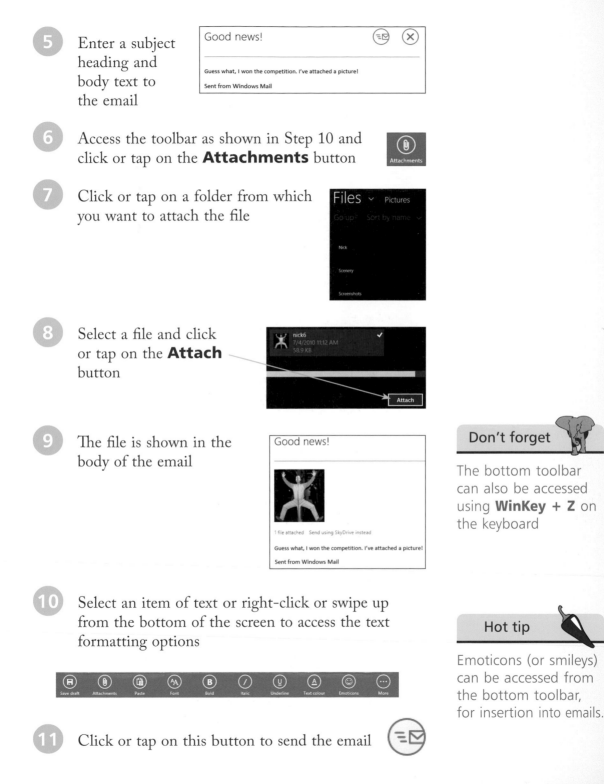

5 Enter a subject heading and body text to the email

Good news!

Guess what, I won the competition. I've attached a picture!

Sent from Windows Mail

6 Access the toolbar as shown in Step 10 and click or tap on the **Attachments** button

Attachments

7 Click or tap on a folder from which you want to attach the file

Files ˅ Pictures

Go up Sort by name ˅

Nick

Scenery

Screenshots

8 Select a file and click or tap on the **Attach** button

nick6
7/4/2010 11:12 AM
58.9 KB

Attach

9 The file is shown in the body of the email

Good news!

1 file attached   Send using SkyDrive instead

Guess what, I won the competition. I've attached a picture!

Sent from Windows Mail

Don't forget

The bottom toolbar can also be accessed using **WinKey + Z** on the keyboard

10 Select an item of text or right-click or swipe up from the bottom of the screen to access the text formatting options

Save draft Attachments Paste Font Bold Italic Underline Text colour Emoticons More

Hot tip

Emoticons (or smileys) can be accessed from the bottom toolbar, for insertion into emails.

11 Click or tap on this button to send the email

Sharing with Mail

It is great to share items via email, whether it is photos, music or video clips. There is no share function directly from Mail (although items can be added with the Attachments option) but items can be shared directly via email through their own apps and the Share Charm. To do this:

 1 Open an item you want to share, such as an image in the **Photos** app

2 Access the **Share Charm**

3 Select the **Mail** app as the method for sharing the item

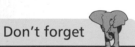
4 The photo is attached to an email in the Mail app. Enter a recipient and subject and send in the same way as a regular email

6 It's a Digital World

Windows 8 makes it easy to work with digital media on your laptop, using the new Photo, Music, Video and Games apps. This chapter shows how to work with these apps so that you can fully immerse yourself in the digital world.

Importing Photos

The Photos app makes it easy to transfer pictures from a camera, scanner, media card reader or pen drive. For each device, you connect it to your computer and then use the Import function in the Photos app. This is an example using a pen drive:

1 Plug the pen drive into a USB port on the computer

2 Click or tap on the **Photos** tile on the Start screen

3 Right-click on the Photos app home screen and click or tap on the **Import** button on the toolbar at the bottom of the screen

4 Click or tap on the device from which you want to import photos

Choose a device to import from

If you don't see your device listed, make sure your device is turned on and connected to your PC.

PEN DRIVE (F:)

Import

5 By default, all available photos are selected, which is depicted by a tick in the top right-hand corner of each photo and a blue border

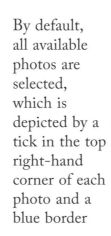

PEN DRIVE (F:) 668 files Clear selection

668 files will be imported to this folder

Olympic Torch   Import   Cancel

6   If you do not want to import all of the photos, click or tap on the **Clear selection** button

7   If you want to re-select all of the available photos, click or tap on the **Select all** button

8   If nothing is selected, right-click on individual photos to select them

125

9   Enter a name for the new folder into which the photos will be downloaded and click or tap on the **Import** button

668 files will be imported to this folder

Olympic Torch   ×   Import   Cancel

10   Once the photos have been downloaded click or tap on the **Open album** button to view the photos

Done!

15 files were imported to Pictures Library\Olympic Torch

Open album

Viewing Photos

Once photos have been downloaded they can be viewed within the Photos app. To do this:

1 Click or tap on the **Photos** tile on the Start screen

2 The available photo libraries are displayed on the Photos Home page. Click or tap on the **Pictures library** button to view photos from your own computer's picture library

3 All of the available albums are displayed, with a thumbnail image from each folder

4 Click or tap here to move back up one level to the Home page

5 Right-click on the Pictures library page to access the toolbar on the bottom of the screen

6 Move the cursor over the bottom right-hand corner of the screen and click or tap on the minus sign to minimize the viewing size of the album thumbnails. This can make it easier to navigate around your albums

Hot tip

Click or tap on the minus sign again in Step 6 to further minimize the screen to view more thumbnails.

Pictures library 3 folders

Bulgaria   Nick   Wildlife

Don't forget

To maximize the screen back to full size, click or tap on the plus sign button in the bottom right-hand corner of the screen.

127

7 Click or tap on an album to view the photos within it

Pictures library 3 folders

Bulgaria   267   Nick   20

...cont'd

8 Move the cursor over the bottom of the screen and use the scroll bar to move through the photos

128

9 As with viewing albums on the previous level up in the Photos app, click or tap on the minus sign to minimize the thumbnails to view more photos

10 Right-click on an image to select it, so that a tick shows in the top right-hand corner

11 When photos are selected the toolbars are displayed at the bottom of the screen. Use these to, from left to right, clear the selection, delete the photo, view all of the photos in the album as a slideshow, select all the photos in the album and import more photos

12 Click or tap on an image to view it at full size. Click or tap here at the left and right of the photo to move to the next or previous full-sized photo

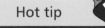

Hot tip

Right-click on a full-sized photo to access the toolbar at the bottom of the screen and the **Back** button at the top. Click or tap on the minus sign in the bottom right-hand corner to return to thumbnail view.

Photo Options

As with other Windows 8 apps there is a range of settings that can be applied to the Photos app. To access these:

1 With the Photos app open, move the cursor over the bottom right-hand corner of the screen and click or tap on the **Settings Charm**

2 At the top of the panel are the settings and options that are specific to the photos app. Click or tap on the **Options** link to access the relevant Photos settings

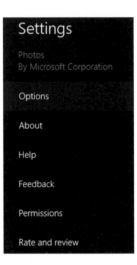

3 The available Photos settings are: Shuffle photos on the app tile, which rotates the photos on the tile on the Start screen (if Live Tile is turned on); Show photos and videos from Pictures library, SkyDrive, Facebook, Flickr and Devices (this determines what is displayed on the Home page of the Photos app)

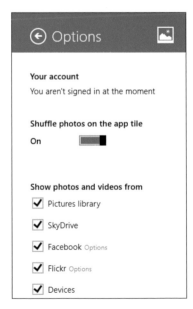

Using Online Services

Within the Photos app you can also access any photos that you have saved on social media sites such as Facebook and Flickr. They can then be viewed in the same way as viewing photos from your picture libraries. To do this:

1 Open the Photos app and click or tap on one of the options on the Home screen (in this example, Facebook)

2 The Photos app will contact the selected service and ask for permission to connect to it. You will have to enter the details with which you normally log in to this service

3 Complete the requested information and click or tap on the **Allow** button to enable sharing between the Photos app and the selected service

131

Beware

If you deactivate an account such as Facebook or Flickr, the photos from there will no longer be available in the Photos app.

4 Once you have connected to the service it will be available on your Photos Home screen. Click or tap on the relevant button to view the photos within it

Playing Music

The Music app is used to access the Xbox Music Store. From here you can preview, buy and download music from the store and also listen to your own music that you have on your computer.

1 Click or tap on the **Music** tile on the Start screen

2 You have to sign-in with a Microsoft Account to view the full features of the Xbox Music Store. Once you have done this you will be signed in automatically each time

3 Preview items are shown on the home screen. Click or tap on the **Xbox Music Store** link to view its contents

4 Browse through the store with the categories in the left-hand panel. Click or tap on an item to preview it

5 Once you have selected an item you can preview individual tracks, view information about the artist, and buy albums or specific tracks

Playing your own music

If you have music copied to your computer (see page 134) you can add this to the Music app and play it through this. To do this:

1 Access the Xbox Music Store through the Music app and scroll to the left-hand side of the store

2 Click or tap on the **Open or play something** link

3 Select the items that you want to include. These will be added to the My Music section in the Music app

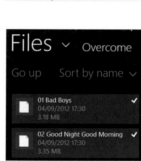

4 Click or tap on the **Open** button

5 The tracks are added to the My Music section in the Music app. Click or tap on items, e.g. an album cover, to see the full contents. Click or tap on this button to play all items in the My Music section

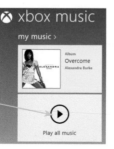

6 To add more items, click or tap on the My Music link above, access the bottom toolbar and click or tap on the **Open file** button and add items as in Step 3

133

Hot tip

When playing music, access the bottom toolbar to use the playback controls. These include Shuffle, Repeat, Previous, Pause and Next. To do this, right-click or swipe up from the bottom of the screen.

Copying Music

As well as buying music from the Music Store, it is also possible to copy music from a CD onto your computer. This is done through the Windows Media Player and once it has been copied it can then be added to your library in the Music app. To copy music with Windows Media Player:

1 Click or tap on the **Windows Media Player** app from the All apps section on the Start screen

2 Insert a CD, which will appear as a disc in the Library pane

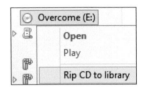

3 Right-click on the CD name and click or tap on the **Rip CD to library** link

4 The files are copied (ripped) from the CD to your Music library within Media Player

5 Click or tap on the Music heading in the Library pane to view the items that have been copied to Media Player

6 Click or tap on the Music library in File Manager. The music that has been copied into Media Player is also available here and this is where it can be accessed by the Music app

Viewing Videos

For movie lovers, the Video app performs a similar purpose to the Music one. It connects to the Xbox Video Store from where you can preview and purchase your favorite movies and TV shows.

135

 Click or tap on the **Video** tile on the Start screen

 You have to sign in with a Microsoft Account to view the full features of the Xbox Video Store. Once you have done this you will be signed in automatically each time

 Preview items are shown on the home screen. Scroll left and right to view more items

 Scroll to the right and click or tap on the **Movies Store** link to view the full range of movies available

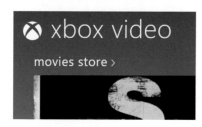

 Click or tap on an item to see more information, view a preview clip and buy and download the movie

Beware

By default, movie DVDs can't be played on Windows 8 laptops. To do this you have to download and buy an enhanced version of the Windows Media Player from the Microsoft website.

Hot tip

If you download movies from the Xbox Video Store to your Xbox you can then use this to view them on your TV.

Don't forget

You can add your own video clips to the Videos app, from the Videos library in File Manager, in the same way as adding your own music to the Music app.

Finding People

An electronic address book is always a good feature to have on a computer and with Windows 8 this function is provided by the People app. This not only allows you to add your own contacts manually; you can also link to any of your online services, such as Facebook, Twitter and LinkedIn, and import the contacts that you have here. To do this:

1 Click or tap on the **People** tile on the Start screen

2 Click on the **Settings Charm** and click or tap on the **Accounts** link

3 The current accounts linked to the People app are listed. Click or tap on the **Add an account** link

4 Select the account or service from which you would like to import your contacts

5 When you connect to the selected service you will be asked to grant Microsoft access to this account

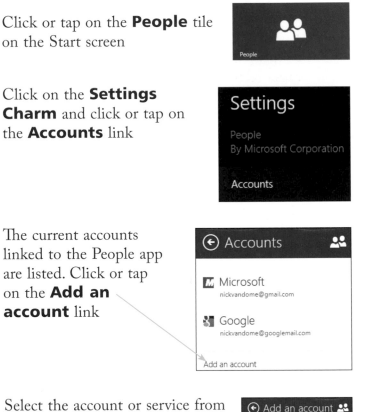

Adding contacts manually

As well as importing contacts, it is also possible to enter them manually into the People app:

To delete a contact, click or tap on them to view their details. Then access the bottom toolbar and click or tap on the **Delete** button to remove the contact.

1 Right-click in the People window, or swipe up from the bottom of the window and click or tap on the **New** button

2 Enter details for the new contact, including name, email address and phone number

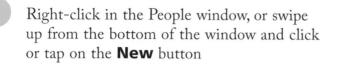

3 Click or tap on the plus sign next to a field to access additional options for that item

The photo for your own details within the People app is taken from the one provided for your Microsoft Account.

4 Click or tap on the **Save** button to create the new contact

5 Click or tap on a contact in the People window to view their details

If you select to edit your own details, you will be taken to your Microsoft Account profile on the Profile Live site.

6 To edit a contact's details, right-click or swipe up from the bottom of the window and click or tap on the **Edit** button. This brings up the same window in Step 2, on the previous page, where the details can be edited

Chatting with Messaging

As long as you have a Microsoft Account, you can use the Messaging app to have text chats with other users of Messaging and also other compatible messaging services. You can also connect to other services and add your contacts for messaging.

1 Click or tap on the **Messaging** tile on the Start screen

2 Access the **Settings Charm** and click or tap on the **Accounts** link

3 Click or tap on the **Add an account** link, or

4 On the Messaging home screen, click or tap on one of the items to add to your account

5 Complete the registration screens to connect to the selected service and add your contacts so that you can message them when they are online

Starting to message

You can send messages to other people if they are online and using a compatible messaging service.

 The current conversations are listed in the left-hand pane of the Messaging window

Don't forget

To delete a conversation thread, right-click on the window, or swipe up from the bottom of the screen, to access the bottom toolbar and click or tap on the **Delete** button.

2 The items in a conversation thread are shown in the main window area

3 Right-click or swipe up from the bottom of the screen to access the toolbar and click or tap on the **New message** button to create a new conversation

4 The New message option opens up the People app from where you can select from all of your contacts or only the ones currently online

5 On the toolbar, click or tap on the **Status** button to select your status as it will appear for others when you are messaging them, or when they are looking to invite you to a new conversation

Don't forget

You can also invite other people to chat, through the Messenger section of the online Profile Live website. To do this, access the bottom toolbar and click or tap on the **Invite** button and click or tap on the **Add a new friend** link. On the Profile Live page, enter the email address of the person you want to invite.

Using the Calendar

The Calendar app can be used to include important events and reminders. To view the calendar:

 Click or tap on the **Calendar** tile on the Start screen

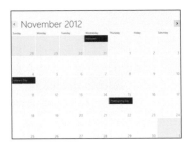 The calendar is displayed by default in month view, with some events and holidays already included. Click or tap on an item to view its details

Click, tap or swipe here to move backwards or forwards through the calendar

 Right-click or swipe up from the bottom of the screen to access the toolbar. Click or tap on this button to view the current day

Click or tap on these buttons to view different formats for the calendar

Adding events

Events can be added to the calendar and various settings can be applied to them such as recurrence and reminders.

 Click or tap on a date and click or tap on the **New** button to create a new event

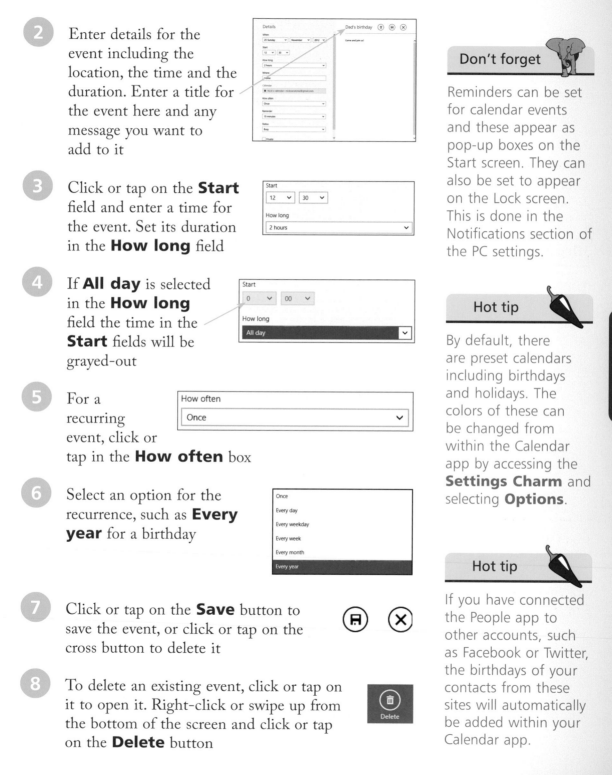

2 Enter details for the event including the location, the time and the duration. Enter a title for the event here and any message you want to add to it

3 Click or tap on the **Start** field and enter a time for the event. Set its duration in the **How long** field

4 If **All day** is selected in the **How long** field the time in the **Start** fields will be grayed-out

5 For a recurring event, click or tap in the **How often** box

6 Select an option for the recurrence, such as **Every year** for a birthday

7 Click or tap on the **Save** button to save the event, or click or tap on the cross button to delete it

8 To delete an existing event, click or tap on it to open it. Right-click or swipe up from the bottom of the screen and click or tap on the **Delete** button

141

Don't forget

Reminders can be set for calendar events and these appear as pop-up boxes on the Start screen. They can also be set to appear on the Lock screen. This is done in the Notifications section of the PC settings.

Hot tip

By default, there are preset calendars including birthdays and holidays. The colors of these can be changed from within the Calendar app by accessing the **Settings Charm** and selecting **Options**.

Hot tip

If you have connected the People app to other accounts, such as Facebook or Twitter, the birthdays of your contacts from these sites will automatically be added within your Calendar app.

Playing Games

The Games app can be used with the Xbox 360 games console. It can be used to play games, join friends for multi-player games, watch TV shows and movies and listen to music. It links into a number of services so that you can access content from places such as YouTube and Netflix. To use the Games app:

1 Click or tap on the **Games** tile on the Start screen

Don't forget

When you first log in to the Games app you will be given a gametag, which will be used to identify you on the Xbox games site.

142

2 You have to log in with your Microsoft Account details. Enter these and click or tap on the **Continue** button

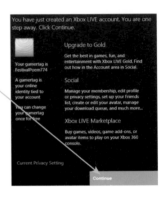

3 Click or tap on a game to preview it and play it

Hot tip

You can also log in to the Xbox site at www.xbox.com to download games and find other people with whom to play games.

4 The Xbox website gives you access to a range of additional content

Sharing with SkyDrive

Cloud computing is now a mainstream part of our online experience. This involves saving content to an online server connected to the service that you are using, i.e. through your Microsoft Account. You can then access this content from any computer, using your account login details, and also share it with other people by giving them access to your cloud service. It can also be used to back up your files, in case they are corrupted or damaged on your PC.

The cloud service with Windows 8 is SkyDrive; you can use it if you have a Microsoft Account.

 Click or tap on the **SkyDrive** tile on the Start screen

 The SkyDrive folders are displayed. Click or tap on one to view its contents, or add files

 Right-click or drag up from the bottom of the screen to view the SkyDrive toolbar at the bottom of the screen

Don't forget

Items can be shared with Windows and Mac users.

 Click or tap on the **Upload** button to add files to the active folder

...cont'd

5 Navigate to the files that you want to add to SkyDrive and click or tap on them to select them

6 Click or tap on this button **Add to SkyDrive**

7 The selected files are added to the active SkyDrive folder

Sharing from SkyDrive

To share files from SkyDrive:

1 Access the **Share Charm**

2 Select items by right-clicking on them. Select a method for sharing, such as **Mail** for sending an email

3 The email contains a link to the SkyDrive folder. The recipient will be able to use this to access the folder and download the items within it

7 On Vacation

Laptops are ideal for taking on vacation and this chapter looks at the issues of taking your laptop with you and keeping it safe.

Transporting Your Laptop

When you are going on vacation your laptop can be a valuable companion. It can be used to download vacation photographs from a digital camera, download home movies from a digital video camera, keep a diary of your vacation, and keep a record of your itinerary and important documents. In many parts of the world it can access the Internet via wireless hotspots so that you can view the Web and send emails. However, when you are traveling with your laptop it is sensible to transport this valuable asset as safely and securely as possible. Some of the options include:

Laptop case

A standard laptop case is a good option for when you are on vacation; it is compact, lightweight and designed to accommodate your laptop and its accessories.

Metal case

If you are concerned that your laptop may be in danger of physical damage on your vacation you may want to consider a more robust metal case. These are similar to those used by photographers and, depending on its size and design, you may also be able to include your photographic equipment.

Backpacks

A serious option for transporting your laptop on vacation is a small backpack. This can either be a standard backpack or a backpack specifically designed for a laptop. The latter is clearly a better option as the laptop will fit more securely and there are also pockets designed for accessories:

Don't forget

A backpack for carrying a laptop can be more comfortable than a shoulder bag as it distributes the weight more evenly.

Keeping Your Laptop Safe

By most measures, laptops are valuable items. However, in a lot of countries around the world their relative value can be a lot more than it is to their owners: in some countries the value of a laptop could easily equate to a month's, or even a year's, wages. Even in countries where their relative value is not so high they can still be seen as a lucrative opportunity for thieves. Therefore it is important to try and keep your laptop as safe as possible when you are on vacation. Some points to consider in relation to this are:

- If possible, try to keep your laptop with you at all times, i.e. transport it in a piece of luggage that you can carry rather than having to put it into a large case

- Never hand over your laptop, or any other of your belongings, to any local who promises to look after them

- If you do have to detach yourself from your laptop, try to put it somewhere secure such as a hotel safe

- When you are traveling, try to keep your laptop as unobtrusive as possible. This is where a backpack carrying case can prove useful as it is not immediately apparent that you are carrying a laptop

- Do not use your laptop in areas where you think it may attract undue interest from the locals, particularly in obviously poor areas. For instance, if you are in a local cafe the appearance of a laptop may create unwanted attention for you. If in doubt, wait until you get back to your hotel

- If you are accosted by criminals who demand your laptop then hand it over. No piece of equipment is worth suffering physical injury for

- Make sure your laptop is covered by your vacation insurance. If not, get separate insurance for it

- Trust your instincts with your laptop. If something doesn't feel right then don't do it

Hot tip

Save your important documents, such as vacation photos, onto a pen drive or CD/DVD on a daily basis when on vacation and keep this away from your laptop. This way you will still have these items if your laptop is lost or stolen.

Temperature Extremes

Traveling means seeing different places and cultures but it also invariably involves different extremes of temperature: a visit to the pyramids of Egypt can see the mercury in the upper reaches of the thermometer, while a cruise to Alaska would present much colder conditions. Whether it is hot or cold, looking after your laptop is an important consideration in extremes of temperature.

Heat

When traveling in hot countries the best way of avoiding damage to your laptop is to prevent it from getting too hot in the first place:

- Do not place your laptop in direct sunlight

- Keep your laptop insulated from the heat

- Do not leave your laptop in an enclosed space, such as a car. Not only can this get very hot, but the sun's power can be increased by the vehicle's glass

Cold

Again, it is best to try to avoid your laptop getting too cold in the first place and this can be done by following similar precautions as for heat. However, if your laptop does suffer from extremes of cold, allow it to warm up to normal room temperature again before you try to use it. This may take a couple of hours, but it will be worth the wait, rather than risking damaging the delicate computing elements inside.

Beware

If a laptop gets too hot it could buckle the plastic casing, making it difficult to close.

Hot tip

Try wrapping your laptop in something white, such as a t-shirt or a towel, to insulate it against the heat.

Laptops at Sea

Water is the greatest enemy of any electrical device, and laptops are no different. This is of particular relevance to anyone who is taking their laptop on vacation near water, such as on a cruise. This not only has the obvious element of water in the sea but also the proliferation of swimming pools that are a feature of cruise ships. If you are going on vacation near water then bear in mind the following:

- Avoid water. The best way to keep your laptop dry is to keep it away from water whenever possible. For instance, if you want to update your diary or download some photographs, then it would be best to do this in an indoor environment, rather than sitting around the pool

- Keeping dry. If you think you will be transporting your laptop near water then it is a good precaution to protect it with some form of waterproof bag. There is a range of "dry-bags" that are excellent for this type of occasion and they remain waterproof even if fully immersed in water. These can be bought from outdoor suppliers

- Drying out. If the worst does occur and your laptop does get a good soaking then all is not lost. However, you will have to ensure that it is fully dried out before you try to use it again

Power Sockets

Different countries and regions around the world use different types of power sockets, and this is an issue when you are on vacation with your laptop. Wherever you are going in the world it is vital to have an adapter that will fit the sockets in the countries you intend to visit. Otherwise you will not be able to charge your laptop.

There are over a dozen different types of plugs and sockets used around the world, with the four most popular being:

North America, Japan

This is a two-point plug and socket. The pins on the plug are flat and parallel.

Hot tip

Power adapters can be bought for all regions around the world. There are also kits that provide all of the adapters together. These provide connections for anywhere worldwide.

Continental Europe

This is a two-point plug and socket. The pins are rounded.

Australasia, China, Argentina

This is a three-point socket that can accommodate either a two- or a three-pin plug. In a two-pin plug, the pins are angled in a V shape.

UK

This is a three-point plug. The pins are rectangular.

Airport Security

Because of the increased global security following terrorist attacks such as those of September 11, 2001, the levels of airport security have been greatly increased around the world. This has implications for all travelers, and if you are traveling with a laptop this will add to the security scrutiny which you will face. When dealing with airport security when traveling with a laptop there are some issues that you should always keep in mind:

- Keep your laptop with you at all times. Unguarded baggage at airports immediately raises suspicion and it can make life very easy for thieves

- Carry your laptop in a small bag so that you can take it on board as hand luggage. On no account should it be put in with your luggage that goes in the hold

- X-ray machines at airports will not harm your laptop. However, if anyone tries to scan it with a metal detector, ask them if they can inspect it by hand instead

- Keep a careful eye on your laptop when it goes through the X-ray conveyor belt and try to be there at the other side as soon as it emerges. There have been some stories of people causing a commotion at the security gate just after someone has placed their laptop on the conveyor belt. While everyone's attention (including yours) is distracted, an accomplice takes the laptop from the conveyor belt. If you are worried about this you can ask for the security guard to hand-check your laptop rather than putting it on the conveyor belt

- Make sure the battery of your laptop is fully charged. This is because you may be asked to turn on your laptop to verify that it is just that, and not some other device disguised as a laptop

- When you are on the plane, keep the laptop in the storage area under your seat, rather than in the overhead locker, so that you know where it is at all times

Beware

If there is any kind of distraction when you are going through security checks at an airport it could be because someone is trying to divert your attention in order to steal your laptop.

Hot tip

When traveling through airport security, leave your laptop in Sleep mode so that it can be powered up quickly if anyone needs to check that it works properly.

Making Telephone Calls

Just because you are on vacation it does not mean that you cannot keep in touch with family and friends at home, and telephone calls via your laptop are an ideal way to do this. As long as you have access to the Internet you can make telephone calls around the world, using an app called Skype. Once this has been downloaded, you can make free telephone calls to anyone else who has Skype on their computer, and cheap ones to landlines or cell phones.

Downloading Skype

To download Skype ready for use on your laptop:

 Access the Skype homepage at www.skype.com

 Click or tap on this button to start the download process

3 Click or tap on the **Save File** button to continue. Follow the wizard to install Skype

Don't forget

Skype is free to download and works with all major computer operating systems, such as Windows, Mac OS X and Linux.

Don't forget

Once Skype has been downloaded it is available on the All apps section of the Start screen.

Adding contacts

Before you start making telephone calls with Skype you have to add the contacts you want to call. To do this:

1 Click or tap on this icon to launch Skype

2 In the Skype window, click or tap on the **Contacts** tab to view details of any current Skype contacts

Contacts	Recent

Search

All ▾

Skype Test Call

captain.tarmac

Euan Turner

3 To add details of another Skype user that you know, click or tap on the **Add Contact** button

Contacts Conversation

Add Contact...

4 Enter the Skype name of the person you want to contact and click or tap on the **View** button

Full name Euan Turner   5 matches found. View

5 Select the person you want to add as a contact

Euan Turner
United Kingdom
Add contact

6 Click or tap on the **Add contact** button

Don't forget

Before you start using Skype you can test your sound through the **Skype Test Call** option in the Skype window.

Don't forget

When you first launch Skype, you have to create a new account by entering your name, a Skype name, a password and an email address.

153

...cont'd

Making a call

To make a telephone call to another Skype user:

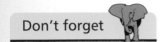
154

1 In the Skype window, click or tap on the **Contacts** tab

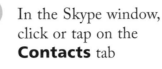

2 Click or tap on a contact name

3 Click or tap on the green **Call Phone** button to make the call. The other user has to accept the call once it has been made to activate it. They do this by clicking on their Answer button

4 Click or tap on the red telephone icon to end the call (this can be done by either user)

5 Click or tap on the **Call phones** button to make a call by entering a specific telephone number

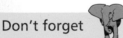

8 Sharing with Your Family

This chapter shows how different people can securely share your laptop.

About Multiple Users

Because of the power and flexibility that is available in a laptop computer, it seems a waste to restrict it to a single user. Thankfully, it is possible for multiple users to use the same laptop. One way to do this is simply to let different people use the laptop whenever they have access to it. However, since everyone creates their own files and documents, and different people use different types of apps, it makes much more sense to allow people to set up their own user accounts. This creates their own personal computing area that is protected from anyone else accessing it. User accounts create a sense of personalization, and also security as each account is protected by a password.

Without user accounts, the laptop will display the default account automatically. However, if different user accounts have been set up on the laptop, a list of these accounts will be displayed when the computer is turned on:

The relevant user can then click on their own account to access it. At this point they will have to enter their password to gain access to their own account. A user can have a local account or a Microsoft Account. If it is the latter, the user will have access to a selection of Microsoft services, through the Windows 8 apps. A password is required for either a local account or a Microsoft one. To see how to add new user accounts see pages 160–161.

Don't forget

If no other user accounts have been set up, yours will be the only one, and you will be the administrator, which means that you can set up new accounts and alter a variety of settings on the laptop.

Customization

Once individual accounts have been set up, it is possible for each individual user to customize their account, i.e. to set the way in which their account appears and operates. This means that each user can set their own preferences, such as for the way the Start screen appears:

The Desktop environment can also be customized. This is done within the **Appearance and Personalization** section of the Control Panel. From here, select the **Personalization** option.

157

Managing Your Account

If you are going to be using multiple user accounts, then you will be able to specify some settings for your own account. By default, you are the administrator of the computer, which means that you have the access permissions to set up accounts and edit their settings. In the Users section of PC settings it is possible to manage your own account, including changing from a Microsoft Account to a local one, changing your password and creating a picture password instead. To do this:

Beware

If you do not protect your own user account with a password, anyone with access to your laptop will be able to view your personal files and information.

1. Access the PC settings from the Settings Charm and click or tap on the **Users** button

PC settings

Personalize

Users

2. Click or tap on the **Switch to local account** button to use a local account as your default when you sign in

Your account

Nick Vandome
nickvandome@gmail.com

You can switch to a local account, but

Switch to a local account

3. Enter your current Microsoft Account sign-in password before you can switch to a local account

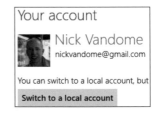

Switch to a local account

You can use an account on this PC only, instead of signing in with your Microsoft account. Save your work now, because you'll need to sign out to do this.

First, we need to verify your current password.

Nick Vandome
nickvandome@gmail.com

Current password

4. Click or tap on the **Next** button

Next

5. Enter a User name and password for your local account

Switch to a local account

Enter the following information. You'll sign in to Windows with a local account from now on.

User name   Nick1   ✕

Password

Reenter password

Password hint

6 To change your password, for either account, click or tap on the **Change your password** button

Sign-in options

Change your password

Create a picture password

Hot tip

When creating or changing a password there is also an option for changing the image that is used to illustrate your account. This can be changed to one of the library images, or you can select one of your own photographs from your hard drive.

7 Enter your password and enter it again to confirm it

Change your Microsoft account password

Nick Vandome
nickvandome@gmail.com

Old password ••••••••

Forgot your password?

New password ••••••••

Passwords must have at least 8 characters and contain at least two of the following: uppercase letters, lowercase letters, numbers, and symbols.

Reenter password

8 Click or tap on the **Next** button to complete the change of password

Next

159

9 Click or tap on the **Create a picture password** button to create this

Sign-in options

Change your password

Create a picture password

Don't forget

Once you have set a password for yourself you will have to enter it every time you turn on your laptop.

10 If you want to create a picture password you have to have a touch screen device. Select a picture with the **Choose picture** button and draw a pattern to create a picture password

Welcome to picture password

Picture password is a new way to help you protect your touchscreen PC. You choose the picture — and the gestures you use with it — to create a password that's uniquely yours.

When you've chosen a picture, you "draw" directly on the touchscreen to create a combination of circles, straight lines, and taps. The size, position, and direction of your gestures become part of your picture password.

Choose picture

Cancel

Adding Users

If more than one person uses the computer, each person can have a user account defined with a user name and a password. To create a new user account, as either a Microsoft Account, or as a local account:

1 Access the PC settings and click or tap on the **Users** button

2 Under **Other users**, click or tap on the **Add a user** button

3 To add a user with a Microsoft Account, enter an email address

4 Click or tap on the **Next** button (see Step 10)

5 To create a local account, click or tap on the **Sign in without a Microsoft account** link

6 At this stage you will still be encouraged to log in with a Microsoft Account, and information about both types is displayed

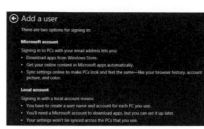

7 Click or tap on the **Local account** button

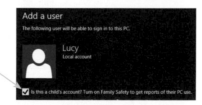

8 Enter a user name, a password and a password hint in case the password is forgotten

9 Select this box if it is a child's account and you want it to be monitored by the **Family Safety** feature

10 For a Microsoft Account, more information is required. Enter the relevant details in the fields and select the **Next** button to complete the additional pages in the registration process

Hot tip

A Guest Account can be enabled within the **User Accounts, Manage Accounts** section of **User Accounts and Family Safety** in the Control Panel. Click or tap on the **Guest** button and click or tap on the **Turn on** button to activate it.

161

Hot tip

Family Safety settings can be applied in the **Family Safety** section in the Control Panel. It is accessed under the **User Accounts and Family Safety** section. Click or tap on a user and then settings can be applied for items such as web filtering, time controls and app restrictions. See pages 162–168 for more details.

Family Safety

Once multiple user accounts have been set up it is possible to apply separate security settings to different accounts. This can be particularly useful if you are going to be setting up an account for grandchildren and you want to have a certain amount of control over how they use the laptop. To do this:

1 Access the **Users Accounts and Family Safety** section of the Control Panel

2 Click or tap on the **Family Safety** link

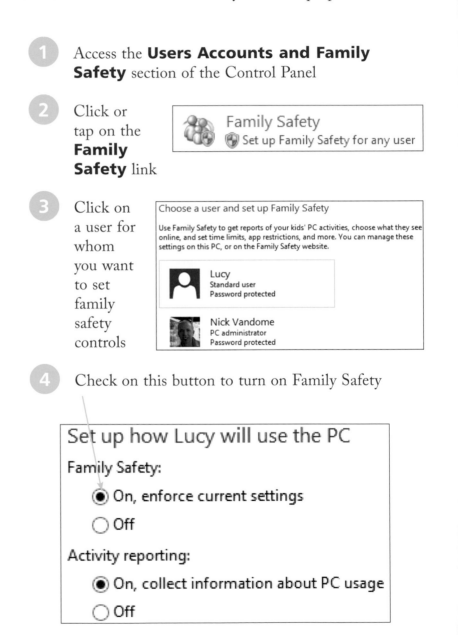

3 Click on a user for whom you want to set family safety controls

4 Check on this button to turn on Family Safety

Web controls

In Windows 8, family safety web controls are performed through the Family Safety section of the Control Panel. To set web controls here:

1 Access the Family Safety section in the Control Panel as shown on the previous page. Click or tap on a user to access their **User Settings**

2 In the User Settings window, click or tap on the **Web filtering** link

Windows settings:

Web filtering
Control the websites Lucy can access online

3 Check on this button to allow specific websites for the user selected on the previous page

Which websites can Lucy view?

○ Lucy can use all websites
● Lucy can only use the websites I allow

Allow or block websites by rating and content types

Set web filtering level

Allow or block all websites

Allow or block specific websites

4 Click or tap on the **Set web filtering level** link

Allow or block websites by rating and content types

Set web filtering level

5 Check on one of the appropriate interest levels. This will restrict any inappropriate website for this level

Which websites can Lucy visit?

Choose a web restriction level:

○ Allow list only
The child can view websites on the Allow List. Adult sites are blocked.
Click here to change Allow List.

○ Designed for children
The child can view websites on the Allow list and websites designed for children. Adult sites are blocked.

● General interest
The child can view websites on the Allow list, websites designed for children, and websites from the general interest category. Adult sites are blocked.

○ Online communication
The child can view websites on the Allow list, websites designed for children, and websites from the general interest, social networking, web chat, and web mail categories. Adult sites are blocked.

Don't forget

If you are setting Family Safety for young people, such as grandchildren, make sure you tell them what you have done, so that they do not think you are acting behind their backs.

163

Click or tap on the **Allow or block specific websites** link in the User Settings window

> Allow or block all websites
>
> Allow or block specific websites

7 Enter the web addresses of any websites you want to include and click or tap on the **Allow** button

> Allow or block specific websites for Lucy
>
> Enter a website to allow or block.
>
> www.allowthisone.com | Allow

8 Enter the web addresses of any websites you want to restrict and click or tap on the **Block** button

> Enter a website to allow or block.
>
> www.blockthisone.com | Allow | Block

9 All allowed and blocked websites are shown under their respective headings

> Allow or block specific websites for Lucy
>
> Enter a website to allow or block.
>
> | Allow | Block
>
> Allowed websites: | Blocked websites:
>
> http://allowthisone.com | http://blockthisone.com

Time controls

A familiar worry when young people are using computers is the amount of time that they are spending on them. However, this can also be controlled in the User Settings window for a selected user. To do this:

1 Click on the **Time limits** link to specify times at which a user can use the computer

Windows settings:

Web filtering
Control the websites Lucy can access online

Time limits
Control when Lucy uses the PC

2 Click or tap on the **Set time allowance** link to set the amount of time the laptop can be used each day

Control when Lucy can use the PC

Set the number of hours Lucy can use the PC per day

Set time allowance

3 Click or tap on this button to set time controls and click or tap on these boxes to specify the amount of time allowed for each day

Control how long Lucy can use the PC

○ Lucy can use the PC all day
● Lucy can only use the PC for the amount of time I allow

⌄ Weekdays: Mon - Fri   2 ⌄ hours   30 ⌄ minutes

⌄ Weekend: Sat - Sun   3 ⌄ hours   30 ⌄ minutes

4 Click or tap on this button to select individual time allowances for specific days

⌃ Weekdays: Mon - Fri	2 ⌄ hours	30 ⌄ minutes
Monday	2 ⌄ hours	30 ⌄ minutes
Tuesday	2 ⌄ hours	30 ⌄ minutes
Wednesday	2 ⌄ hours	30 ⌄ minutes

...cont'd

5 Click on the **Set curfew** link to specify times at which a user can, and cannot, use the computer

> Control when Lucy can use the PC
>
> Set the number of hours Lucy can use the PC per day
>
> Set time allowance
>
> Set the time of day Lucy can use the PC
>
> Set curfew

6 Check on this button to specify a time restriction for the selected user

> ## When can Lucy use the PC?
>
> ○ Lucy can use the PC all day
>
> ◉ Lucy can only use the PC during the time ranges I allow

7 Click on the squares for times at which you do not want the specified user to use the computer. The blocked times are colored blue. Drag over a group of squares to select these rather than selecting individual time slots

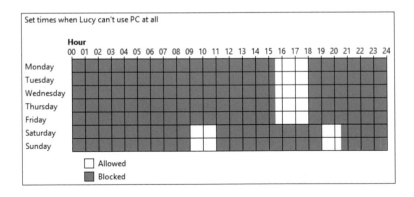

Games and Apps controls

Computer games are another very popular pastime for young people. These include games that are downloaded from the Web and also those that are bought on CDs or DVDs. However, just as with movies, some games are unsuitable for younger children and should have ratings to specify the age groups for which they are suitable. It is then possible to control which games are played. To do this:

Don't forget

Most laptops come with a range of games pre-installed. The content in these is usually suitable for all age groups.

1 Click or tap on the **Windows Store and game restrictions** link to specify the games that a user can use on the computer

Windows settings:

Web filtering
Control the websites Lucy can access online

Time limits
Control when Lucy uses the PC

Windows Store and game restrictions
Control by rating or title

2 Check on this button to restrict the use of games and Windows Store apps

Control which games and Windows Store apps Lucy can use

○ Lucy can play all games and view all Windows Store apps
◉ Lucy can only use games and Windows Store apps I allow

3 Click or tap on the **Set game and Windows Store ratings** link to specify the ratings level of the games and apps that the user can use

Allow or block games and Windows Store apps by rating

Set game and Windows Store ratings

Maximum allowed rating: Parental Guidance (BBFC)

4 Check on a button to specify a ratings level according to the official classifications for your geographic location

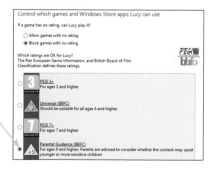

Control which games and Windows Store apps Lucy can use

If a game has no rating, can Lucy play it?

○ Allow games with no rating
◉ Block games with no rating

Which ratings are OK for Lucy?
The Pan European Game Information, and British Board of Film Classification defines these ratings.

PEGI
bbfc

○ **3** PEGI 3+
For ages 3 and higher

○ **U** Universal (BBFC)
Should be suitable for all ages 4 and higher

○ **7** PEGI 7+
For ages 7 and higher

◉ **PG** Parental Guidance (BBFC)
For ages 8 and higher. Parents are advised to consider whether the content may upset younger or more sensitive children

...cont'd

5 Click or tap on the **Allow or block specific games** link to block any of the game apps currently on the laptop

> Allow or block any game on your PC by name
>
> Allow or block specific games
>
> Always blocked: None
> Always allowed: None

6 In the User Settings window, click or tap on the **App restrictions** link

> Windows settings:
>
> Web filtering
> Control the websites Lucy can access online
>
> Time limits
> Control when Lucy uses the PC
>
> Windows Store and game restrictions
> Control by rating or title
>
> App restrictions
> Control the apps allowed on your PC

7 Check on this button to restrict the apps that the selected user can access

> Which apps can Lucy use?
>
> ○ Lucy can use all apps
> ◉ Lucy can only use the apps I allow
>
> Check the apps that can be used:
>
> | File | Description |
> | --- | --- |
> | Windows Store apps | |
> | ☑ Bing | Microsoft Corporation |
> | ☑ Camera | Microsoft Corporation |
> | ☐ Finance | Microsoft Corporation |
> | ☑ Games | Microsoft Corporation |
> | ☐ Mail, Calendar, People and Messaging | Microsoft Corporation |
> | ☑ Maps | Microsoft Corporation |
> | ☑ Music | Microsoft Corporation |
> | ☐ News | Microsoft Corporation |

8 Check on the apps that the user is allowed to access. The rest will be restricted and unavailable

9 Networking and Wireless

Setting up a Network

In computing terms a network is a when a computer is connected to one, or more, computers, or it is connected to the Internet. This means that content and files can be shared between computers.

To set up a network you must first get all of the required hardware in place. For this you will require a router, which is the device through which all of the elements of the network will communicate. To do this:

170

1. Plug in your router to the mains electricity

2. Connect your router to your Internet connection, via either a phone line or a cable. This usually plugs into the back of the router

3. For a cable connection, attach one end of the cable to the computer and the other to the router

4. If you have a laptop with wireless connectivity the laptop will communicate with the router wirelessly when the network software creates the network

5. Connect any other items of hardware that you want to include in the network, such as a printer. This can be done wirelessly, if the printer is equipped with a wireless card, or, more commonly, with a USB or an Ethernet connection

Going Wireless

For networking, "wireless" means connecting your computer to other devices using radio waves rather than cables. These can include a router for connecting to a network, a printer, keyboard, mouse or speakers (as long as these devices also have a wireless capability). For the laptop user in particular, this gives you the ultimate freedom; you can take your laptop wherever you want and still be able to access the Internet and use a variety of peripherals.

Wireless standards

As with everything in the world of computers, there are industry standards for wireless connections: for networking devices the standard is known as IEEE 802.11. The purpose of standards is to ensure that all of the connected devices can communicate with each other.

The IEEE 802.11 standard (or just 802.11) used for networks has a number of different variations (known as protocols) of the original standard. These variations have been developed since the introduction of 802.11 in 1997 with a view to making it work faster and cover a greater range. Early wireless devices used the 802.11a and 802.11b protocols, while the most widely used one at the time of writing is the 802.11n protocol. When you are creating a wireless network it is best to have all of the devices using the same version of 802.11. For instance, if you have a wireless card in your laptop that uses 802.11n then it is best to have the same version in your router. However, most modern wireless cards and routers have multiple compatibility and can cater for at least the b and g versions of the standard. If two devices are using different 802.11 protocols they should still be able to communicate with each other but the rate of data transfer will probably be slower than if both of the devices used the same protocol.

The Bluetooth standard is another method of connecting devices wirelessly. It does not have the same range as 802.11 and is generally now mainly used for connecting cell phones.

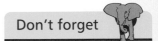

Very few new devices use the 802.11a version of the standard although newer devices will usually be backwards-compatible with it.

Devices using the 802.11n protocol can communicate with each other via radio waves over distances of approximately 25 yards (indoors) and 75 yards (outdoors).

Discover Networks

Connect your computers to form your network, using Ethernet cables and adapters or by setting up your wireless adapters and routers. When you start up each computer, Windows 8 will examine the current configuration and discover any new networks that have been established since the last start up. You can check this, or connect manually to a network, from within the default settings from the Settings Charm. To do this:

Beware

If your network is unavailable there will be a warning on the network button in Step 1.

1 Click or tap on the **Settings Charm** and click or tap on the **Network** button

2 Under the Wi-Fi heading, click or tap on one of the available networks

3 Check on the **Connect automatically** box and click or tap on the **Connect** button to connect to the selected network

4 The selected network is shown as Connected. This is also shown on the Settings Charm in Step 1

Network and Sharing Center

The Network and Sharing Center within the Control Panel is where you can view settings for your network.

Don't forget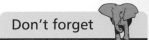

The Network and Sharing Center displays network settings and provides access to networking tasks for the computer.

1 To open the Network and Sharing Center, access the Control Panel and click or tap on the **Network and Internet** link

Network and Internet
View network status and tasks
Choose homegroup and sharing options

2 Click or tap on the **Network and Sharing Center** link

Network and Sharing Center
View network status and tasks | Connect to a network
View network computers and devices

HomeGroup
Choose homegroup and sharing options

Internet Options
Change your homepage | Manage browser add-ons
Delete browsing history and cookies

Hot tip

In the Network and Sharing Center, click or tap on the **Set up a new connection or network** link to create a different network from the one currently in use.

3 Details of the current network are displayed in the Network and Sharing Center

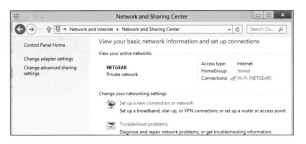

4 Click or tap on the **Connections** link to see details of your Wi-Fi connection

Access type: Internet
HomeGroup: Available to join
Connections: Wi-Fi (NETGEAR)

5 The Wi-Fi information is displayed. Click or tap on the **Properties** button for more information

Wi-Fi Status

General

Connection
IPv4 Connectivity: Internet
IPv6 Connectivity: No Internet access
Media State: Enabled
SSID: NETGEAR
Duration: 03:04:43
Speed: 36.0 Mbps
Signal Quality:

Details... | Wireless Properties

Activity

Sent — Received

Bytes: 17,300,020 | 21,345,167

Properties | Disable | Diagnose

Close

Join the HomeGroup

A HomeGroup is a network function that enables a
Windows 8 computer to connect to another Windows 8
machine (or Windows 7) and share content. There are
different ways to join a HomeGroup, depending on whether
you connect from the Windows 8 interface, or through the
Control Panel.

Connecting through the Windows 8 interface

To connect to a HomeGroup from the Windows 8 interface:

1 Access the **Settings Charm** and
click or tap on the **Change PC
settings** button

Change PC settings

2 Click or tap on the **HomeGroup**
button under PC settings

HomeGroup

3 Under the
HomeGroup
heading, click or
tap on the **Create**
button

HomeGroup

Create a homegroup
With a homegroup you can share libraries and devices with other people on this network.
You can also stream media to devices.

Your homegroup is protected with a password, and you'll always be able to choose what you
share.

Create

4 Specify shared items.
Drag the buttons to
the right to enable
items to be shared
via the HomeGroup

Libraries and devices

When you share content, other homegroup members can see it, but only you can change it.

Documents
Shared

Music
Not shared

Pictures
Shared

Videos
Not shared

Printers and devices
Not shared

Don't forget

Only computers on
the same network and
running the Windows
7 or 8 operating
system (any edition)
will be invited to join
the HomeGroup.

5 Under the
Membership heading
is a password. This has

Membership

If someone else wants to join your homegroup, give them this password:
EF4ct9ZN6P

to be entered on any other computers that want to
join the HomeGroup

Connecting through the Control Panel

To join a HomeGroup from the Control Panel:

1 Access **Network and Internet** in the Control Panel and click or tap on the **HomeGroup** link

2 Click or tap on the **Next** button to start setting up the HomeGroup

3 You can view details of the HomeGroup you want to join. Click or tap on the **Join now** button

4 Select the items that you want to share in the HomeGroup and click or tap on the **Next** button

5 Enter the password that has to be provided from the other computer

6 Once you have joined the HomeGroup you can share files on the other computer and vice versa

Beware

HomeGroup applies to any user with an account on the computer, so if a different user logs on, the associated files will also be accessible.

Don't forget

Windows generates the password when the HomeGroup is created (see page 174). If you forget the password, you can find it in the Control Panel on any computer already joined to the HomeGroup.

Sharing Files and Folders

There are different ways in which you can share items once a HomeGroup has been set up:

1 Open File Explorer and select **Homegroup** in the Library pane and click or tap on the **Share libraries and devices** button in the Share section of File Explorer

2 Select the items that you want to share with the HomeGroup. This will be done automatically, i.e. if you share Pictures then all of the items in the Pictures library will be shared, as will new ones that are added

3 To share a specific item, select it in File Explorer and click or tap on the **Homegroup** button in the Share section

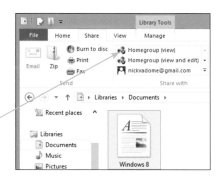

4 Select the **Homegroup** in the Navigation pane of the File Explorer Library pane to view the shared item in Step 3

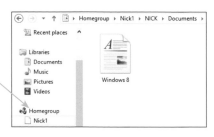

Sharing Settings

Within the Network and Sharing Center there are also options for specifying how items are shared over the network, not just in the HomeGroup. To select these:

1 Open the Network and Sharing Center and click or tap on the **Change advanced sharing settings** link

> Change advanced sharing settings

2 Select sharing options for different networks, including private, guest or public and all networks. Options can be selected for turning on network discovery so that your computer can see other ones on the network, and file and printer sharing

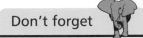

Don't forget

If you are sharing over a network you should be able to access the Public folder on another computer (providing that network discovery is turned on). If you are the administrator of the other computer you will also be able to access your own home folder, although you will need to enter the required password for this.

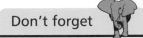

3 Click or tap on these buttons to view the options for each network category

Saving Files for Sharing

When you want to save files so that other people on your network can access them (other than with the HomeGroup) this can be done by either saving them into the Public folder on your own laptop, or saving them into the Public folder of another computer on your network. To do this:

1 Create the file that you want to save onto the network

2 First, save the file to a folder within your own file structure, i.e. one that is within the File Explorer Libraries, not on the network. This will ensure that you always have a master copy of the document

3 Select **File>Save As** from the Menu bar (this is standard in most types of apps)

4 The Save As window has options for where you can save the file

Don't forget

Files can also be copied to Public folders on the network by dragging and dropping them from within your own file structure. This can be done within the File Explorer window.

5 Click or tap on the **Network** icon in the left-hand pane

6 Double-click or tap on the Public folder on your laptop if this is where you want to save the file; or

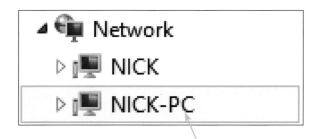

7 Double-click tap on another computer on the network to save the file here

8 Double-click or tap on the **Users** folder, then the **Public** folder

Beware

If you copy files to your own Public folder, other computers on the network will only be able to access these when your laptop is turned on.

179

9 Double-click or tap on the folder into which you want to save the file

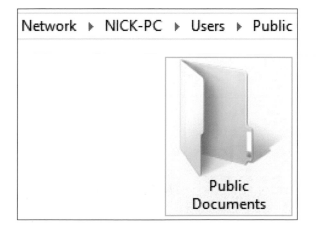

Sharing a Printer

When you join a HomeGroup, Windows may detect a shared printer. However, the software drivers required may not be installed on this machine. To make the printer available

1 Click or tap on the **Install printer** button

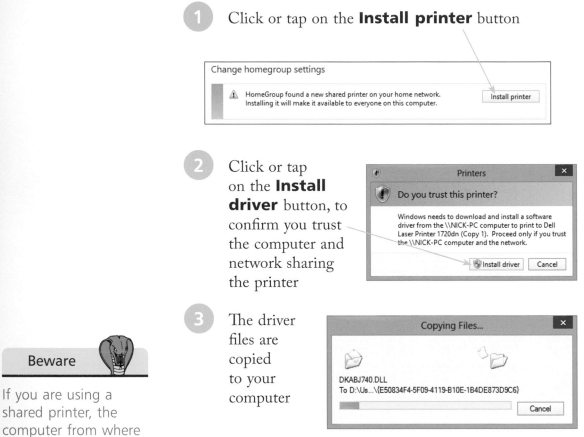

Change homegroup settings

⚠ HomeGroup found a new shared printer on your home network.
Installing it will make it available to everyone on this computer.

Install printer

2 Click or tap on the **Install driver** button, to confirm you trust the computer and network sharing the printer

Printers ✕

🛡 Do you trust this printer?

Windows needs to download and install a software driver from the \\NICK-PC computer to print to Dell Laser Printer 1720dn (Copy 1). Proceed only if you trust the \\NICK-PC computer and the network.

🛡 Install driver   Cancel

3 The driver files are copied to your computer

Copying Files... ✕

DKABJ740.DLL
To D:\Us...\{E50834F4-5F09-4119-B10E-1B4DE873D9C6}

Cancel

Beware

If you are using a shared printer, the computer from where you are sharing it has to be turned on in order for you to use the printer.

4 The shared printer is added to the Devices and Printers section in the Control Panel

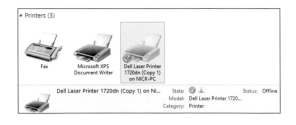

▲ Printers (3)

Fax   Microsoft XPS Document Writer   Dell Laser Printer 1720dn (Copy 1) on NICK-PC

Dell Laser Printer 1720dn (Copy 1) on NI...   State: ✓ 🖶   Status: Offline
Model: Dell Laser Printer 1720...
Category: Printer

View Network Components

You can also view the network components in the network in File Explorer. To do this:

1 Open File Explorer and click or tap on the **Network** link

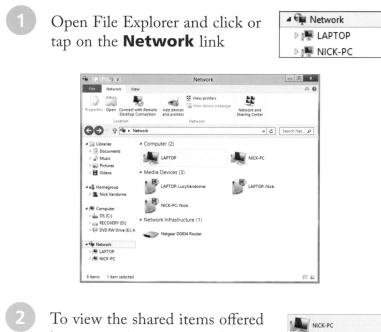

2 To view the shared items offered by a particular computer, for example the Nick-PC, double-click or tap on the associated icon

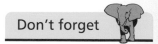

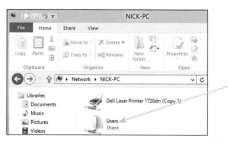

3 Double-click or tap to view the contents of networked folders

Public files and folders plus those belonging to the currently-active user are available for access. Items can be copied here for sharing.

181

Don't forget

The Public folder on your own computer can be used to make items available to other users on the same network.

Network Troubleshooting

If you have problems on your network, you can try to resolve them with the Troubleshoot options. To do this:

1 Open the Network and Sharing Center and select **Troubleshoot problems**

> Troubleshoot problems
> Diagnose and repair network problems, or get troubleshooting information.

2 Windows searches online for troubleshooting packs

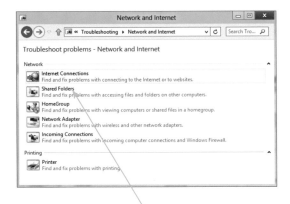

3 Select, for example, Shared Folders and follow the prompts to describe and hopefully resolve the issue

10 Battery Issues

Types of Battery

A laptop's battery is one of the items that helps to define its identity: without it, the portable nature of the laptop would be very different as it would always have to be connected with a power cable. Laptops have used a variety of different types of batteries since they were first produced and over the years these have become smaller, lighter and more powerful. However, laptop batteries are still relatively heavy and bulky and are one of the major sources of weight in the machine:

Don't forget

The type of battery provided with a laptop, and the approximate lifespan for each charge, should be displayed with the details about the machine on the manufacturer's website or in the promotional literature that comes with it.

The types of batteries used in modern laptops are:

- Lithium-ion. This is a type of battery that has a good weight-to-power ratio and loses its charge at a relatively slow rate. However, they can be prone to overheating if they are not treated properly or are defective

- Lithium polymer. This is an advanced version of the lithium-ion battery. It is generally considered to be a more stable design

Don't forget

The quality of laptop batteries is improving all the time. Some models currently on the market have a battery life of up to six or even eight hours.

These types of batteries are rechargeable and so they can be used numerous times once they initially run out. However, all rechargeable batteries eventually wear out and have to be replaced.

Power Consumption

Battery life for each charge of laptop batteries is one area on which engineers have worked very hard since laptops were first introduced. For most modern laptops the average battery life for each charge is approximately between three and five hours. However, this is dependent on the power consumption of the laptop, i.e. how much power is being used to perform particular tasks. Power-intensive tasks will reduce the battery life of each charge cycle. These types of tasks include:

- Watching a DVD (this requires the enhanced version of the Windows Media Player)

- Editing digital video

- Editing digital photographs

When you are using your laptop you can always monitor how much battery power you currently have available. This is shown by the battery icon that appears at the bottom right on the Taskbar:

Because of the vital role that the battery plays in relation to your laptop it is important to try to conserve its power as much as possible. To do this:

- Where possible, use the mains adapter rather than the battery when using your laptop

- Use the Sleep function when you are not actively using your laptop

- Use power-management functions to save battery power (see pages 186–188)

Beware

If you are undertaking an energy-intensive task, such as watching a DVD, try to use the external AC/DC power cable rather than the battery, otherwise the battery may drain very quickly and the laptop will close down.

Battery Management

Unlike desktop computers, laptops have options for how the battery is managed. These allow you to set things like individual power schemes for the battery and to view how much charge is left in the battery. This can be done from the Control Panel. To access the options for managing your laptop's battery:

1   Access the **Control Panel**

2   Click or tap on the **Hardware and Sound** link

Hardware and Sound
View devices and printers
Add a device
Adjust commonly used mobility settings

3   Click or tap on the **Power Options** link

Power Options
Change battery settings
Change what the power buttons do
Require a password when the computer wakes
Change when the computer sleeps
Adjust screen brightness

Power Plans

The Power Options window displays the available settings for balancing battery usage and your laptop's performance. Select the buttons to change to a different power plan:

...cont'd

System Settings

Within the Power Options window it is possible to select settings for how the laptop operates when the Power or the Sleep button is pressed, or when the lid is closed. To do this:

1 In the Power Options window, click or tap on one of these links to apply the settings for each item

> Choose what the power buttons do
>
> Choose what closing the lid does
>
> Create a power plan
>
> Choose when to turn off the display

2 The options are displayed in **System Settings**

3 Click or tap on these boxes to select an action for each item, either on battery power or when plugged in

Beware

If you don't protect your laptop with a password for when it is woken from sleep, anyone could access your folders and files if they wake the laptop from sleep.

187

4 Click or tap on the **Change settings that are currently unavailable** link to access more options

 Change settings that are currently unavailable

5 Check on the additional options and click or tap on the **Save changes** button to apply them

Shutdown settings
- ☑ **Turn on fast startup (recommended)**
  This helps start your PC faster after shutdown. Restart isn't affected. Learn More
- ☑ **Hibernate**
  Show in Power menu.
- ☑ **Lock**
  Show in account picture menu.

Save changes

Hot tip

One of the options in Step 5 is **Hibernate**, which will appear on the Power button if this is selected here.

...cont'd

Editing plan settings
To edit the settings for a specific power plan:

1 Click or tap on one of the options in the Power Options window and click or tap on the **Change plan settings** link

Plans shown on the battery meter

◉ **Balanced (recommended)**   Change plan settings
Automatically balances performance with energy consumption on capable hardware.

2 Select options for turning off the display when the laptop is not being used and when the computer goes to sleep, and also the display brightness, either on battery power or when the laptop is plugged in

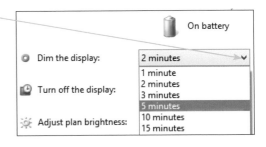

3 Click or tap on these buttons to make selections for each item

4 Click or tap on the **Save changes** button

Charging the Battery

Laptop batteries are charged using an AC/DC adapter, which can also be used to power the laptop instead of the battery. If the laptop is turned on and being powered by the AC/DC adapter, the battery will be charged at the same time, although at a slower rate than if it is being charged with the laptop turned off.

The AC/DC adapter should be supplied with a new laptop and consists of a cable and a power adapter. To charge a laptop battery using an AC/DC adapter:

1. Connect the AC/DC adapter and the cable and plug it into the mains socket

2. Attach the AC/DC adapter to the laptop and turn on at the mains socket

3. When the laptop is turned on the Power Meter icon is visible at the bottom right of the Taskbar. Double-click on this to view the current power details

Don't forget

A laptop battery can be charged whether the laptop is turned on or off.

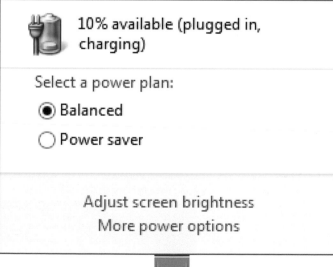

Removing the Battery

Although a laptop's battery does not have to be removed on a regular basis, there may be occasions when you want to do this. These include:

- If the laptop freezes, i.e. you are unable to undertake any operations using the keyboard or mouse and you cannot turn off the laptop using the power button

- If you are traveling, particularly in extreme temperatures. In situations such as this you may prefer to keep the battery with you to try to avoid exposing it to either very hot or very cold temperatures

To remove a laptop battery:

1 With the laptop turned off and the lid closed, turn the laptop upside down

2 Locate the battery compartment and either push or slide the lock that keeps the battery in place

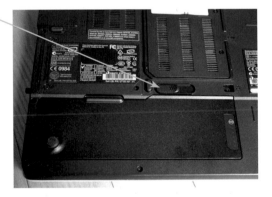

Don't forget

To re-insert the battery, or a new battery, push it gently into the battery compartment until it clicks firmly into place.

3 Slide the battery out of its compartment

Dead and Spare Batteries

No energy source lasts forever and laptop batteries are no exception to this rule. Over time, the battery will operate less efficiently until it will not be possible to charge the battery at all. With average usage, most laptop batteries should last approximately five years, although they will start to lose performance before this. Some signs of a dead laptop battery are:

- Nothing happens when the laptop is turned on using just battery power

- The laptop shuts down immediately if it is being run on the AC/DC adapter and the cord is suddenly removed

- The Battery Meter shows no movement when the AC/DC adapter is connected, i.e. the Battery Meter remains at 0% and shows as not charging at all

Beware

If you think that your battery may be losing its performance, make sure that you save your work at regular intervals. Although you should do this anyway, it is more important if there is a chance of your battery running out of power.

> 0% available (plugged in, not charging)
>
> Select a power plan:
> ● Balanced
> ○ Power saver
>
> Adjust screen brightness
> More power options

Spare battery

Because of the limited lifespan of laptop batteries it is worth considering buying a spare battery. Although these are not cheap it can be a valuable investment, particularly if you spend a lot of time traveling with your laptop and you are not always near a source of mains electricity. In situations such as this a spare battery could enable you to keep using your laptop if your original battery runs out of power.

When buying a spare battery, check with the laptop's manufacturer that it will be compatible: in most cases the manufacturer will also be able to supply you with a spare battery for your laptop.

Battery Troubleshooting

If you look after your laptop battery well it should provide you with several years of mobile computing power. However, there are some problems that may occur with the battery:

- **It won't keep its charge even when connected to an AC/DC adapter.** The battery is probably flat and should be replaced

- **It only charges up a limited amount.** Over time, laptop batteries become less efficient and so do not hold their charge so well. One way to try to improve this is to drain the battery completely before it is charged again

- **It keeps its charge but runs down quickly.** This can be caused by the use of a lot of power-hungry applications on the laptop. The more work the laptop has to do to run applications, such as those involving videos or games, the more power will be required from the battery and the faster it will run down

- **It is fully charged but does not appear to work at all when inserted.** Check that the battery has clicked into place properly in the battery compartment and that the battery and laptop terminals are clean and free from dust or moisture

- **It is inserted correctly but still does not work.** The battery may have become damaged in some way, such as becoming very wet. If you know the battery is damaged in any way, do not insert it, as it could short-circuit the laptop. If the battery has been in contact with liquid, dry it out completely before you try inserting it into the laptop. If it is thoroughly dry it may work again

- **It gets very hot when in operation.** This could be caused by a faulty battery and it can be dangerous and lead to a fire. If in doubt, turn off the laptop immediately and consult the manufacturer. In some cases, faulty laptop batteries are recalled, so keep an eye on the manufacturer's website to see if there are any details of this if you are concerned

Don't forget

If there is no response from your laptop when you turn it on in battery mode, try removing the battery and re-inserting it. If there is still no response then the battery is probably flat and should be replaced.

192

Hot tip

If you are not going to be using your laptop for an extended period of time, remove the battery and store it in a safe, dry, cool place.

11 Troubleshooting

Viruses are the scourge of the computing world and this chapter shows how to best defend against any malicious software. It also covers updating your system software and backing up your data.

Protecting Against Viruses

One of the most important considerations for any computer user is to make sure that they have suitable protection against malicious software that can infect their machine and compromise its operation and potentially damage or erase folders and files. Windows 8 comes with some built-in protection against viruses, malware and spyware (see following pages) but it is also a good idea to have additional protection in the form of anti-virus software. There are several products on the market and three to look at are:

- McAfee at www.mcafee.com

- Norton at www.norton.com

- Kaspersky at www.kaspersky.com

Using anti-virus software
Most anti-virus software works in a similar way:

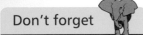

Don't forget

When you buy an anti-virus app you will usually have to pay an annual subscription. This will enable you to keep downloading the latest virus protection files (definitions) to combat new viruses as they appear.

Beware

New viruses are being released all the time so it is important that you scan for them on a daily basis.

1 Open your chosen app to access its features. Click or tap on an item to see its options

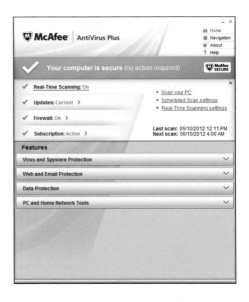

2 Click on the **Scan your PC** button to perform a scan for viruses on your laptop

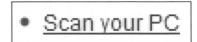

3 The progress of the scan, along with any potential problems, is displayed as it is taking place

Completed	✻ **Quick Scan in progress**	✕
29%	Items: 1092	
	Scanning: C:\Windows\system32\itircl.dll	

[Scan in background] [Cancel] [Pause]

Don't forget

If any viruses are discovered you will be given options for how to deal with them.

4 Once a successful scan has taken place you will be informed of issues, if any

Issues	**Quick Scan complete**	✕
0	✓ McAfee did not detect any issues on your PC. No further action is required.	
	Next scheduled scan: 06 October 2012 04:00	

[Done]

5 Click on the **Updates** button to get the latest virus definitions, i.e. the means to stop the latest viruses that have been identified. Updates can usually be set to be performed automatically

✓ Scan: Complete >

✓ **Updates: Current**

✓ Firewall: On >

✓ Subscription: Active >

Internet and networks

Anti-virus software can also warn you about potential unwanted access to your laptop from the Internet or another user on a network:

1 Click or tap on the **Web and Email Protection** option to select options for ensuring your laptop is as safe as possible when accessing the Internet

Features

Virus and Spyware Protection ⌄

Web and Email Protection ⌃

Firewall: **On**
Firewall protects your PC against intruders who can hijack your PC or steal personal information, and polices the information your PC sends and receives. Learn more

SiteAdvisor: **Installed**
SiteAdvisor provides website ratings and reports that tell you which sites are safe and which aren't—before you visit them.

Using a Firewall

A firewall is a program that can be used to help stop malicious programs, such as viruses and spyware, from entering your laptop. It acts like a barrier around your laptop and aims to repel any items that it does not trust (these usually come from the Web).

Firewalls can be purchased along with anti-virus software but there is also one that comes pre-installed with Windows 8. To use this:

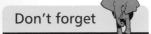

Don't forget

If you have an anti-virus app it will probably also have its own firewall. This will take over from the Windows Firewall.

1 Access the **Control Panel** and click or tap on the **System and Security** link

> **System and Security**
> Review your computer's status
> Save backup copies of your files with File History
> Find and fix problems

2 Click or tap on the **Windows Firewall** link

> **Windows Firewall**
> Check firewall status
> Allow an app through Windows Firewall

3 By default, the firewall should be turned on, i.e. protecting your laptop

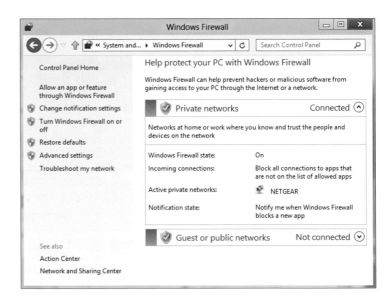

4 Select **Allow an app or feature through Windows Firewall,** to view the allowed apps

Allow an app or feature through Windows Firewall

5 Check on these boxes to allow specific apps and features to be allowed through the Firewall

6 Select **Allow another app**, if you want to allow an app through the Firewall

7 Click or tap on an app to select it

8 Click or tap on the **Add** button

Beware

If you turn off the firewall you will keep getting system messages telling you that you should turn it back on again.

197

Windows Defender

Another option for stopping malicious software entering your laptop is Windows Defender, which can check for spyware and similar types of programs. To use this:

1 Access the Control Panel and type *Defender* in the Search box and select **Windows Defender**

2 The Windows Defender window contains details for scanning your laptop and viewing the results

3 Click or tap on the **Scan now** button to perform a scan on your laptop

Scan now

4 Once the scan is completed the following message will appear if no malicious items are detected

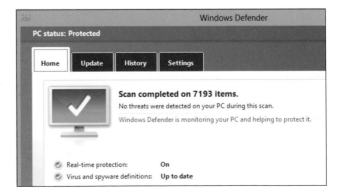

5 Click or tap on the **Update** tab to update your virus and spyware items. This is done automatically but it can also

be performed manually by clicking or tapping on the **Update** button

6 Click on the **History** tab to view the previous results from the scans that have been undertaken. Click or tap on the **View details** button to see the scan results

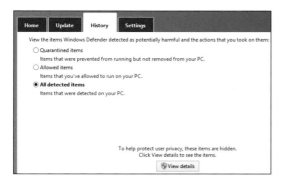

7 Click or tap on the **Settings** tab and click or tap here to select options for how Windows Defender operates. Select the **Real-time protection** option to activate automatic alerts if malicious software tries to access your laptop

Don't forget

If any items are quarantined you will be given options for how to deal with them and remove them from your laptop.

User Account Controls

One of the features in Windows 8 that is aimed at stopping malicious files or apps being downloaded onto your laptop is called the User Account Controls. This produces a warning window when a variety of actions are performed, such as certain apps being run. However, after time this can become counterproductive: the window can appear so frequently that it is okayed without thinking, just to get rid of it. If this becomes too annoying, it is possible to disable the User Account Controls so that the warning windows do not appear. To do this:

 Access the **Control Panel** and click or tap on the **System and Security** link

System and Security
Review your computer's status
Save backup copies of your files with File History
Find and fix problems

Under the Action Center section, click or tap on the **Change User Account Control settings** link

Action Center
Review your computer's status and resolve issues
Change User Account Control settings
Troubleshoot common computer problems

Drag this slider to specify the level at which you want the user controls set. The higher the setting, the more security warnings will appear while you are using your laptop

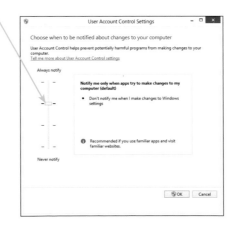

Beware

If you turn off the User Account Controls your computer may be more vulnerable to infection from unauthorized apps. However, if you have anti-virus software running, this should pick up any of these problems.

Action Center

For all of the security settings on your laptop it is useful to be able to see them in one location. This can be done with the Action Center, which also enables you to alter these settings if required. To use the Action Center:

1 Access the **Control Panel** and click or tap on the **System and Security** link

System and Security
Review your computer's status
Save backup copies of your files with File History
Find and fix problems

2 Click or tap on the **Action Center** link

Action Center
Review your computer's status and resolve issues
Change User Account Control settings
Troubleshoot common computer problems

3 All of the current essential security settings are displayed

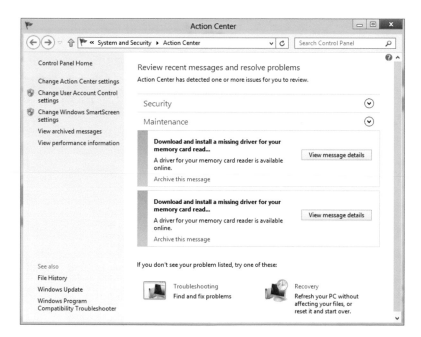

Don't forget

An item with a green banner is fully protected and up-to-date. An amber banner means that there are some issues relating to this item. A red banner means that the required settings are not in place and your laptop could be at risk.

Updating Software

One of the best ways to try to keep your laptop as secure as possible is to make sure that your system software is fully up to date. This is because there are frequent updates that repair security problems that come to light with the operating system and associated programs. With Windows 8, updates can be downloaded and installed automatically through the use of the Windows Update function:

1 Access the **Control Panel** and click or tap on the **System and Security** link

2 Click or tap on the **Windows Update** link

3 The Windows Update window displays any updates that are available and when updates were last checked for and installed

Don't forget

Updates are released on a regular basis so you should be looking for new ones on a weekly basis at least.

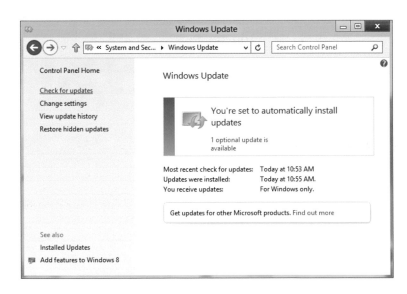

4 For some updates you will be prompted to restart your laptop so that the updates can be installed

Hot tip

Even if you have updates installed automatically it is a good idea to check frequently to see which updates have been installed.

5 Click or tap on the **Check for updates** link to manually check for new updates

> Control Panel Home
>
> Check for updates

6 Click or tap on the **Change settings** link to alter how Windows Update operates

> Control Panel Home
>
> Check for updates
> Change settings

7 By default, updates are scheduled to be downloaded and installed automatically

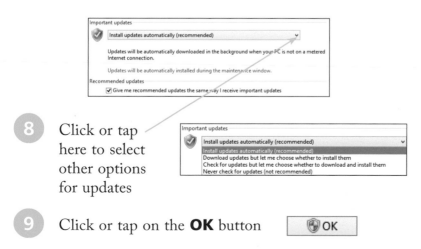

8 Click or tap here to select other options for updates

9 Click or tap on the **OK** button ⬛ OK

Backing Up

The security settings in Windows 8 are designed to try to protect your laptop as much as possible and ensure that you don't lose any valuable data. However, no system is infallible and sometimes malicious programs, or human error, can cause the loss of files and documents on your laptop. Because of this, it is important that you have a robust procedure in place for backing up your information and also have the means to restore it if it does get deleted or corrupted. The first step is to make sure your computer files are backed up. To do this:

Don't forget

Backing up means copying your data to another location. One of the best options for doing this is to use an external hard drive.

1. Open the **Control Panel** and select **Save backup copies of your files with File History** in the **System and Security** category

   System and Security
   Review your computer's status
   Save backup copies of your files with File History
   Find and fix problems

2. The first time you do this, you can select a drive such as an external hard drive or a network drive to use for the backup

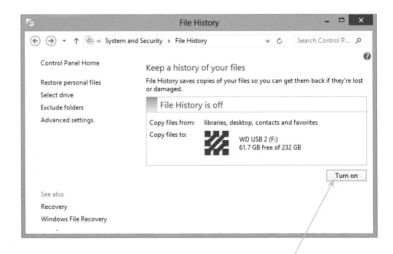

3. Click or tap on the **Turn on** button to back up copies of your files

204

4 The backup runs and copies the files to the selected location, i.e. the external drive

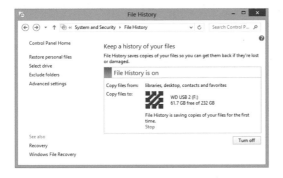

5 Click or tap on the **Run now** link to perform another backup

WD USB 2 (F:)
61.7 GB free of 232 GB

Files last copied on 07/09/2012 10:30.
Run now

6 Click or tap on the **Advanced settings** link to select additional options for how the backup is performed

Control Panel Home

Restore personal files

Select drive

Exclude folders

Advanced settings

7 Select any additional options and click or tap on the **Save changes** button at the bottom of the window

Advanced settings

Choose how often you want to save copies of your files, and how long to keep saved versions.

Versions

Save copies of files:	Every hour (default) ∨
Size of offline cache:	5% of disk space (default) ∨
Keep saved versions:	Forever (default) ∨

Clean up versions

Restoring Files

Once files have been backed up they should be kept in a safe place, preferably in a different location from the original files, i.e. the laptop itself. If the original files ever get deleted or corrupted, they can be restored from the backup location. To do this:

Beware

Depending on the types of files that you have selected for backing up, the process can take a considerable amount of time, so be prepared for a wait.

---

1 Open the **Control Panel** and click or tap on the **File History** section

2 Click or tap on the **Restore personal files** button

Control Panel Home

Restore personal files

3 The files for the current date are displayed

4 Click or tap here to move back to an earlier date, if you want to restore files from here

5 Select the items you want to restore by clicking or tapping on them. (Double-click or tap on a folder to view its contents and select individual files)

Hot tip

If you are at all worried about copying over existing files, restore the files from the backup disc to a different location from the original one.

6 Click or tap on this button to restore the selected items

7 If there is a file conflict with the ones that you are restoring, i.e. there is one with the same name already in the selected location, you will be presented with options for what to do with the files being restored

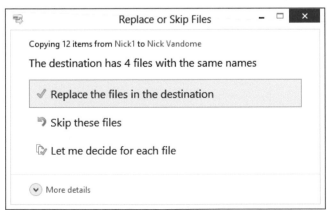

System Restore

Inevitably when working with your laptop you will come across occasions when it behaves erratically. This could be because of a program that has been loaded or software (driver) that has been loaded for an external device, such as a printer. However, with Windows 8 it is possible to try to rectify the problem by restoring the settings of your laptop to an earlier date. This does not affect any of your personal files or folders, but it can help the laptop perform better by taking it back to a date before the problem started. To use System Restore you have to first create a Restore Point from where you can then restore your settings:

Hot tip

System Restore is a good option to use if your laptop starts to perform erratically after you have installed a new app.

1 Access the **Control Panel** and click or tap on the **System** link

2 Click or tap on the **System protection** link, to access this section within the System Properties window

3 Click or tap on the **Create** button, to create a restore point manually

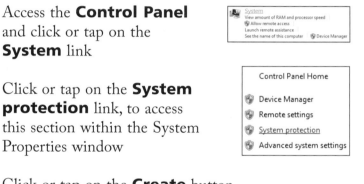

4 Enter a title for the restore point

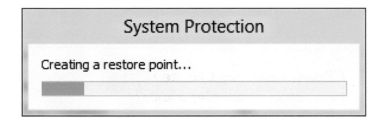

Hot tip

Always start with the most recent System Restore point to see if this fixes the problem. If not, use a more distant restore point.

5 Click or tap on the **Create** button

6 The required data is written to the disk and the manual restore point is set up

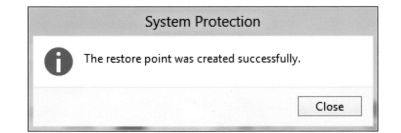

7 Once the restore point has been created, click or tap on the **Close** button

...cont'd

Using Restore Points

The installation of a new app or driver software may make Windows behave unpredictably or have other unexpected results. Usually, uninstalling the app or rolling back the driver will correct the situation. If this does not fix the problem, you can use an automatic or manual restore point to reset your system to an earlier date when everything worked correctly.

Hot tip

Whenever you install a new app, or a driver for an external device, it is always worth creating a custom restore point, so that you have a dated reference for everything you have added to your laptop.

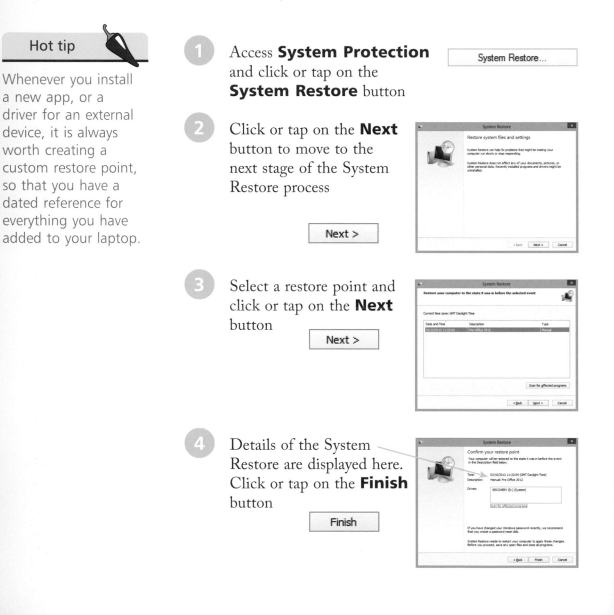

1 Access **System Protection** and click or tap on the **System Restore** button

2 Click or tap on the **Next** button to move to the next stage of the System Restore process

3 Select a restore point and click or tap on the **Next** button

4 Details of the System Restore are displayed here. Click or tap on the **Finish** button

Index